THE
ESSENTIAL
Rottweiler

Consulting Editor
IAN DUNBAR, PH.D., MRCVS

Featuring Photographs by
RENÉE STOCKDALE

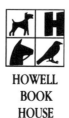

HOWELL
BOOK
HOUSE

Howell Book House

A Simon & Schuster Macmillan Company

1633 Broadway

New York, NY 10019

Macmillan Publishing books may be purchased for business or sales promotional use. For information please write: Special Markets Department, Macmillan Publishing USA, 1633 Broadway, New York, NY 10019.

Library of Congress Cataloging-in-Publication Data

The essential Rottweiler / featuring photographs by Renée Stockdale.

    p. cm.

   ISBN 0-87605-343-6

   1. Rottweiler dog.   I. Howell Book House

SF429.R7E84   1998   98-3133

636.73—dc21   CIP

Manufactured in the United States of America

10 9 8 7 6 5 4 3 2

Series Directors: Dominique DeVito, Don Stevens

Series Assistant Director: Jennifer Liberts, Amanda Pisani

Editorial Assistant: Michele Matrisciani

Photography Editor: Sarah Storey

Book Design: Paul Costello

Photography:

  Front cover photo by Close Encounters of the Furry Kind/J. Harrison; back cover photo by George Shagawat.

  Courtesy of Diana Robinson: 73, 76, 77

  All other photos by Renée Stockdale.

  Many Rottweilers in interior photos courtesy of Peggy Johnson, Rottweilers with Unbeatable Temperaments, Willis, MI.

Production Team: Chris Van Camp, Jenaffer Brandt, Linda Quigley

CHAPTER ONE

Getting to Know Your Rottweiler

Properly bred and well-reared Rottweilers share many similarities. These include a strong desire to work, whether it be at carrying things around the house or pulling a small cart; a playful, exuberant character; a protective nature that can manifest itself in possessiveness; and a deep loyalty to their family. By nature, guard dogs are loyal, intelligent, strong and have great endurance.

Rottweiler owners cannot be reminded often enough that this

1

able or allowed to express these traits properly. An intelligent dog is going to become bored and frustrated quickly if he is confined to a small space and left unsupervised for hours at a time. A strong dog, if not trained in the fundamentals of house manners, which include responding to "Sit," "Down," "Stay," "Come," "Heel," "Wait," "Off," "No" and many other commands, may end up inadvertently bullying his owners.

As their responsibility to this magnificent breed, today's Rottweiler owners must take on a commitment to respect his characteristics and allow him to develop and use them appropriately. Basic training from puppyhood is the first, easiest, most fun and most rewarding way to channel his energy.

Basic training from puppyhood is essential to your Rottweiler's development.

dog was developed to work; he was bred to be a take-charge dog, and is so to this day.

What today's owners need to keep in mind is that intelligence, strength and a deep sense of loyalty can work against a dog who is not

CHARACTERISTICS OF THE ROTTWEILER

territorial

playful

loving with family

happiest when he's got a "job" to do

Give Your Dog a Job

The Rottweiler possesses great intelligence. Owners are obliged to utilize that intelligence by interacting with the dog. With proper training and guidance, the Rottweiler will be very obedient; however, he was bred to make independent decisions and take independent action. As a dog bred for hard work, the healthy, well-conditioned Rottweiler has boundless energy and stamina (except in hot weather). He will be happier and more content if he has a few simple jobs to do. Carrying your packages, mail or newspaper will afford him great pleasure.

ROTTWEILERS AT PLAY

A most endearing trait of the breed, perhaps in contrast to his strength and determination, is his almost childlike playfulness. Rottweilers can entertain themselves for hours lying on their back, spinning a ball or other toy between their forepaws.

Adolescent Rottweilers can be quite rowdy and boisterous. Rottweilers can be taught to be respectful as they reach maturity; however, their exposure to small children, the very elderly or the disabled should never be without supervision.

Usually first-time owners are surprised and delighted to have their Rottweiler youngster voluntarily follow them from room to room. Rottweilers like to have their favorite people in view. When the owner leaves the room, the dog will usually wait a few minutes, anticipating the person's return. If the owner doesn't reappear in what the dog perceives as a reasonable length of time, the dog feels compelled to go seek out that person.

VOCAL ROTTWEILERS

Many Rottweilers are quite vocal in expressing their feelings; in addition to the barking, growling and whining common to all breeds, many Rottweilers appreciate a good songfest and will throw back their

A Rottweiler's endearing playfulness will often last well beyond puppyhood.

A Dog's Senses

Sight—Dogs can detect movement at a greater distance than we can, but they can't see as well up close. They can also see better in less light, but can't distinguish many colors.

Sound—Dogs can hear about four times better than we can, and they can hear high-pitched sounds especially well. Their ancestors, the wolves, howled to let other wolves know where they were; our dogs do the same, but they have a wider range of vocalizations, including barks, whimpers, moans and whines.

Smell—A dog's nose is his greatest sensory organ. His sense of smell is so great, he can follow a trail that's weeks old, detect odors diluted to one-millionth the concentration we'd need to notice them, even sniff out a person under water!

Taste—Dogs have fewer taste buds than we do, so they're likelier to try anything—and usually do, which is why it's especially important for their owners to monitor their food intake. Dogs are omnivores, which means they eat meat as well as vegetable matter like grasses and weeds.

Touch—Dogs are social animals and love to be petted, groomed and played with. To the Rottweiler, the world is his.

heads and howl with vigor. Some Rottweilers (particularly males) will rumble deep in their chests, a sort of purring, to express pleasure at having their tummies scratched or their ears massaged.

RESPONSIBLE OWNERSHIP

The Rottweiler has risen to the number-two position in popularity of all registered dogs. However, this breed is not suitable for casual ownership. Great responsibility and liability can be involved when you share your life with a Rottweiler. If the dog will be left unattended for hours, if you do not have a securely fenced yard where your Rottweiler may safely have some freedom of movement, if you are too busy or too lazy to devote sufficient time to properly rear and train the dog, if you are too permissive to be a disciplinarian, then you would be wise to not get a dog at all.

Many Rottweilers are born thieves and take great delight in acquiring their treasures. To prevent the dog from stealing something that may be damaging to him or distressful to you, it's best to employ the "ounce of prevention" rule.

Many Rottweilers welcome the challenge of a closed door—cupboard, closet, refrigerator, what have you. If you have other dogs or very small children, Rottweilers will be quick to take advantage of this unexpected access to food and forbidden articles. Rotties take great pleasure as well in rolling on objects—a ball, a washcloth, a chew toy, discarded clothing—anything may prompt them to fling themselves on it and have a good roll.

BE YOUR ROTTWEILER'S LEADER

With a dog of such incredible strength of body and will, it is imperative that the owner be the dog's leader. If the dog does not believe you're the boss, you're not. You must at all times display the attitude and presence of a leader. This certainly does not mean brutality in training, nor does it mean shouting and keeping the dog subdued and fearful. It means that in your heart of hearts there must be no doubt that you are fully capable of controlling this animal. You can do this by being sure of what you want and expect from your dog and taking the time to teach him these things.

Make sure your Rottweiler has a job to do; leaving your pet penned up with nothing to do for hours on end will produce behavior problems.

5

CHAPTER TWO

Homecoming

Before you bring your Rottweiler home, you will need some supplies. You don't want to have to make an emergency run to the store at midnight because you forgot something. Some of the supplies are basic, for both the puppy and the adopted adult. Others items are specifically for one or the other.

FIRST THINGS FIRST

Food

Find out what your puppy's breeder has been feeding her and get some of that same food. If you wish to switch to a different brand, do so over a period of time so your Rottweiler can adjust. Rapid changes of foods can result in an upset stomach and diarrhea.

Bowls

You will need a bowl for food and a bowl for water. The food bowl can be just about anything; some people like plastic, others like ceramic or stainless steel. Whatever you use should be large enough to hold 4 to 6 cups of food and should be easy to clean. Change the water and clean the bowl daily, and if your Rottweiler likes to splash in it, check it several times a day to make sure the dog doesn't go thirsty.

Collar and Leash

You will also need a collar and leash for your new Rottweiler. A buckle collar, either with a metal buckle or the plastic quick-release closure, is good for both puppies and adult dogs. Adjustable collars are available that can be made larger as the puppy grows.

You will want an identification tag for your dog's buckle collar. This

PUPPY ESSENTIALS

Your new puppy will need:

food bowl	bed
water bowl	crate
collar	toys
leash	grooming supplies
ID tag	

Crating your dog will help keep her out of trouble while you're away and will give her a safe den-like retreat for sleeping.

tag should include your name and both a daytime and an evening telephone number.

be something the puppy can chew on, because very shortly your puppy will start teething and will have a driving need to chew.

If you are bringing home an older puppy or adult Rottweiler, you will have to offer larger rawhides or indestructible toys. Ask at your local pet store what they have available.

GETTING YOUR HOUSE READY

Prior to bringing home your Rottweiler, you will need to make sure your house is ready. First of all, set up the crate in your bedroom. Many people take away the nightstand next to the bed and put the crate right there. This way your dog will spend six to eight hours close to you and can smell and hear you all night long. This is a great way to bond with the dog, and you don't even have to do anything. Also, if the puppy needs to go outside during the night, you will hear the puppy whine and cry before there is an accident.

Next, decide where your dog will spend her days. If you are home all day, this is not a big problem; you can supervise the puppy when she's out and about. When you can't

A Rottweiler who receives proper training and socialization will be a wonderful addition to the family.

Crate

Your new Rottweiler will need a kennel crate to use as a bed, a place of refuge and a place for quiet time. This crate can be the plastic type that airlines require or it can be a heavy metal wire cage. The style is up to you, but the crate should be large enough for an adult Rottie to stand up, turn around and lie down in comfortably.

Toys

Last, but certainly not least, you will need some toys for your Rottweiler. If you are going to be bringing home a new puppy, the toys should watch the pup, you can put her in her crate. However, if you work outside the home, you will need a secure place, preferably outside.

If you will be leaving your Rottweiler outside, you might want to build her a secure run or exercise area. Make sure your dog won't be able to climb or dig out of it and that other dogs, coyotes or predators can't get in. Your dog will need a house and shelter from the weather, toys and an unspillable water bowl.

Puppy-Proofing

You must make sure your house, yard and garage are safe for your new Rottweiler. In the house, crawl around on your hands and knees and look at things from a dog's viewpoint. Pick up or put away anything

An important task for a new dog owner is puppy-proofing the house.

that looks even remotely interesting. With a young puppy or a new dog in the house, preventing problems from happening is imperative.

If your Rottweiler is going to have access to the garage, make sure all chemicals, paints and car parts are up high, out of reach. Many things, like antifreeze, are very poisonous. By sectioning off the garage and picking up and storing away dangerous substances, you can ensure your dog's safety.

In the yard, look for possible escape routes, places where your dog could go under or over the fence. Again, just as in the house, try to look at your yard from the dog's

point of view. Be sure to put away garden tools, fertilizers, pesticides and pool supplies.

SETTING UP A SCHEDULE

Dogs are creatures of habit and thrive on a regular routine that doesn't vary too much from day to day. Tiny puppies, especially, need a routine. At 8 weeks of age, puppies sleep a lot. Your puppy will eat, relieve herself, play and sleep, and a couple of hours later will repeat the whole cycle. However, as she gets older, she will gradually sleep less and play more. As she learns and

Puppies need chew toys, but you should avoid playing tug-of-war if your puppy is already overly aggressive.

Before allowing unsupervised play, teach your children how to safely handle your new puppy.

develops bowel and bladder control, she will go longer periods between needing to relieve herself, from every hour to every three or four hours.

PREVENTING PROBLEMS

Many of the commonly seen problems with dogs can be avoided through simple prevention. Puppy-proofing your house is one means of prevention. Supervising the dog is another means of prevention. Your Rottweiler can't chew up your sofa if you supervise her while she's in the house with you. When you can't watch her, put her in her crate or outside in her pen with lots of toys. By supervising the dog, you can teach her what is allowed and what is not.

QUALITY TIME WITH YOUR DOG

Rottweilers are very people-oriented dogs and must spend time with their owners. Your dog should be inside with you when you are home and next to your bed at night. In addition, you will need to make time to play with your dog, train her and make sure that she gets enough exercise.

To spend time with your dog in the morning, getting up thirty

HOUSEHOLD DANGERS

Curious puppies and inquisitive dogs get into trouble not because they are bad, but simply because they want to investigate the world around them. It's our job to protect our dogs from harmful substances, like the following:

In the House:

cleaners, especially pine oil

perfumes, colognes, aftershaves

medications, vitamins

office and craft supplies

electric cords

chicken or turkey bones

chocolate

some house and garden plants, like ivy, oleander and poinsettia

In the Garage:

antifreeze

garden supplies, like snail and slug bait; pesticides; fertilizers; mouse and rat poisons

minutes earlier will give you time for a fifteen- to twenty-minute walk before taking your shower. In the evening, take the children with you as you walk the dog; you can find out what's going on with the kids as you exercise and train your dog.

CRATE-TRAINING

Adding a puppy to your household can be a wonderful experience, but it can sour quickly if the puppy is ruining your carpets and chewing up your shoes. There is a training tool that can help—a crate.

A crate allows you to use the dog's natural denning instinct, the instinct that causes dogs to curl up behind the chair or under a table when they nap. Puppies also have a natural instinct not to soil (relieve themselves in) the place where they sleep. A crate helps housetrain a puppy by using that instinct.

Introduce the crate by opening the door and tossing a treat or toy inside. Allow the puppy to come and go as she pleases and to investigate the crate. When she is going in and out after the treat or toy, give her a treat and close the door. Leave the door closed for a few minutes and then let the puppy out if, and only if, the puppy is being quiet.

Put the puppy in her crate when you are home and can't supervise her

Putting your Rottweiler puppy in her crate while you can't keep an eye on her could prevent a potentially life-threatening accident.

or when you are busy, such as eating a meal. Put the puppy in the crate when she is overstimulated—time-outs are good for puppies, too. And, of course, put the puppy in her crate for the night.

Never leave a young puppy in the crate longer than one hour,

Adequate exercise will help use up excess energy that may otherwise lead your Rottweiler to mischief.

Being a good neighbor means keeping your Rottweiler on a leash or behind a fence while she's outside.

except at night when the crate is next to your bed. It takes a while for the puppy to develop good bowel and bladder control, and she will need an opportunity to relieve herself every hour. You may, of course, return your puppy to the crate after her "break."

A puppy will adjust to her new home more quickly when given ample opportunity to rest in peace and quiet.

CHAPTER THREE

To Good Health

The strongest body and soundest genetic background will not help a dog lead a healthy life unless he receives regular attention from his owner. Dogs are susceptible to infections, parasites and diseases for which they have no natural immunity. It is up to us to take preventative measures to make sure that none of these interferes with our dog's health. It may help to think of the upkeep of a dog's health in relation to the calendar. Certain things need to be done on a weekly, monthly and annual basis.

*Run your hands
regularly over
your dog to feel
for any injuries.*

PREVENTIVE HEALTH CARE

Weekly grooming can be the single best monitor of a dog's overall health. The actual condition of the coat and skin and the "feel" of the body can indicate good health or potential problems. Grooming will help you discover small lumps on or under the skin in the early stages before they become large enough to be seen without close examination. You may spot fleas and ticks when brushing the coat and examining the skin. Besides harboring diseases and parasites, they can make daily life a nightmare for some dogs. Many Rotties are severely allergic to even a couple of fleas on their bodies. They scratch, chew and destroy their coat and skin because of fleas. Even if the fleas are not actually seen, their existence can be confirmed by small black specks in the coat.

Flea Control

Flea control is never a simple endeavor. Dogs bring fleas inside, where they lay eggs in the carpeting and furniture—anywhere your dog goes in the house. Consequently, real control is a matter of not only treating the dog but also the other environments the flea inhabits. The yard can be sprayed, and in the house, sprays and flea bombs can be used, but there are more choices for the dog. Flea sprays are effective for one to two weeks, depending on their ingredients. Dips applied to the dog's coat following a bath have equal periods of effectiveness. The disadvantage to both of these is that some dogs may have problems with the chemicals.

*The flea is a
die-hard pest.*

Flea collars can be effective, as they prevent the fleas from traveling to your dog's head, where it's moist and more hospitable. Dog owners tend to leave flea collars on their dogs long after they've ceased to be effective. Again, some dogs may have problems with flea collars, and children should never be allowed to handle them.

Some owners opt for products that can work from the inside out. One option is a pill (prescribed by a veterinarian) that you give to the dog on a regular basis in his food. The chemicals in the pill course through the dog's bloodstream, and when a flea bites, the blood kills the flea.

Another available option is a product that comes in capsule form. The liquid in the capsule is applied near the dog's shoulders, close to the skin, where it distributes into the skin and coat to protect against fleas and ticks. Ask your veterinarian about this nontoxic, long-lasting flea and tick preventative.

Ticks

As you examine your Rottweiler, check also for ticks that may have

Three types of ticks (l–r): the wood tick, brown dog tick and deer tick.

lodged in his skin, particularly around the ears or in the hair at the base of the ear, the armpits or around the genitals. If you find a tick, which is a small insect about the size of a pencil eraser when engorged with blood, smear it with petroleum jelly. As the tick suffocates, it will back out and you can then grab it with tweezers and kill

17

Use tweezers to remove ticks from your dog.

Keeping your Rottweiler clean is an important step in maintaining his health.

it. If the tick doesn't back out, grab it with tweezers and slowly pull it out, twisting very gently. Don't just grab and pull or the tick's head may separate from the body. If the head remains in the skin, an infection or abscess may result and veterinary treatment may be required.

A word of caution: Don't use your fingers or fingernails to pull out ticks. Ticks can carry a number of diseases, including Lyme disease, Rocky Mountain spotted fever and others, all of which can be very serious.

Proper Ear Care

Another weekly job is cleaning the ears. Many times an ear problem is evident if a dog scratches his ears or shakes his head frequently. Clean ears are less likely to develop problems, and if something does occur, it will be spotted while it can be treated easily. If a dog's ears are very dirty and seem to need cleaning on a daily basis, it is a good indication that something else is going on in the ears besides ordinary dirt and the normal accumulation of earwax.

A visit to the veterinarian may indicate a situation that needs special medication.

Keeping Nails Trimmed

The nails on all feet should be kept short enough so they do not touch the ground when the dog walks. Dogs with long nails can have difficulty walking on hard or slick surfaces. This can be especially true of older dogs. As nails grow longer, the only way the foot can compensate and retain balance is for the toes themselves to spread apart, causing the foot itself to become flattened and splayed.

Nails that are allowed to become long are also more prone to splitting. This is painful to the dog and usually requires surgical removal of the remainder of the nail for proper healing to occur.

Keeping Eyes Clear

Rotties' eyes rarely need special attention. A small amount of matter in the corner of the eye is normal, as is a bit of "tearing." Rotties with eyelashes that turn inward and rub against the eye itself often exhibit more tearing than normal due to the irritation to the eyes. These eyelashes can be surgically removed if it appears to be a problem, but are often ignored.

VACCINES

All dogs need yearly vaccinations to protect them from common deadly diseases. The DHL vaccine, which protects a dog from distemper, hepatitis and leptospirosis, is given for the first time at about 7 weeks of age, followed by one or two boosters several weeks apart. After this, a dog

YOUR PUPPY'S VACCINES

Vaccines are given to prevent your dog from getting an infectious disease like canine distemper or rabies. Vaccines are the ultimate preventive medicine: They're given before your dog ever gets the disease so as to protect him from the disease. That's why it is necessary for your dog to be vaccinated routinely. Your veterinarian will put your puppy on a proper schedule and will remind you when to bring in your dog for shots.

When you adopt your Rottweiler, make sure to find our what vaccines he has already received and when he should go back to the vet to have the series completed.

should be vaccinated every year throughout his life.

Since the mid-1970s, parvovirus and coronavirus have been the cause of death for thousands of dogs. Puppies and older dogs are most frequently affected by these illnesses. Fortunately, vaccines for these are now routinely given on a yearly basis in combination with the DHL shot.

Kennel cough, though rarely dangerous in a healthy dog who receives proper treatment, can be annoying. It can be picked up anywhere that large numbers of dogs congregate, such as veterinary clinics, grooming shops, boarding kennels, obedience classes and dog

shows. The Bordatella vaccine, given twice a year, will protect a dog from getting most strains of kennel cough. It is often not routinely given, so it may be necessary to request it.

INTERNAL PARASITES

While the exterior part of a dog's body hosts fleas and ticks, the inside of the body is commonly inhabited by a variety of parasites. Most of these are in the worm family. Tapeworms, roundworms, whipworms, hookworms and heartworms all plague dogs. There are also several types of protozoa, mainly *coccidia* and *giardia*, that cause problems.

The common tapeworm is acquired by the dog eating infected fleas or lice. Normally one is not aware that a healthy dog even has tapeworms. The only clues may be a dull coat, a loss of weight despite a good appetite or occasional gastrointestinal problems. Confirmation is by the presence of worm segments in the stool. These appear as small, pinkish-white, flattened rectangular-shaped pieces. When dry, they look like rice. If segments are not present, diagnosis can be made by the discovery of eggs when a stool sample is examined under a microscope. Ridding a dog temporarily of tapeworms is easy with a worming medicine prescribed by a veterinarian.

Ascarids are the most common roundworm (nematode) found in dogs. Adult dogs that have roundworms rarely exhibit any symptoms that would indicate the worm is in their body. These worms are cylindrical in shape and may be as long as 4 to 5 inches. They do pose a real danger to puppies, where they are usually passed from the mother through the uterus to the unborn puppies.

It is wise to assume that all puppies have roundworms. In heavy infestations they will actually appear in the puppy's stools, though their presence is best diagnosed by a stool sample. Treatment is easy and can begin as early as 2 weeks of age and is administered every two weeks thereafter until eggs no longer appear in a stool sample or dead worms are not found in the stool following treatment. Severely infected puppies can die from roundworm infestation. Again, the worming medication should be obtained through a veterinarian.

Hookworm is usually found in warmer climates, and infestation is generally from ingestion of larvae from the ground or penetration of the skin by larvae. Hookworms can cause anemia, diarrhea and emaciation. As these worms are very tiny and not visible to the eye, their diagnosis must be made by a veterinarian.

Whipworms live in the large intestine and cause few if any symptoms. Dogs usually become infected when they ingest larvae in contaminated soil. Again, diagnosis and treatment should all be done by a veterinarian. One of the easiest ways to control these parasites is by picking up stools on a daily basis. This will help prevent the soil from becoming infested.

The protozoa can be trickier to diagnose and treat. Coccidiosis and

Common internal parasites (l–r): roundworm, whipworm, tapeworm and hookworm.

giardia are the most common, and primarily affect young puppies. They are generally associated with over-crowded, unsanitary conditions and can be acquired from the mother (if she is a carrier), the premises them-selves (soil) or even water, especially rural puddles and streams.

ADVANTAGES OF SPAY/NEUTER

The greatest advantage of spaying (for females) or neutering (for males) your dog is that you are guaranteed your dog will not pro-duce puppies. There are too many puppies already available for too few homes. There are other advantages as well.

Advantages of Spaying

No messy heats.

No "suitors" howling at your windows or waiting in your yard.

Prevents pyometra (disease of the uterus) and decreases incidence of breast cancer.

Advantages of Neutering

Decreases fights, but doesn't affect the dog's personality.

Decreases roaming.

Decreased incidences of urogenital diseases.

The most common symptom of protozoan infection is mucous-like blood-tinged feces. Once diagnosed, treatment is quick and effective, and the puppy returns to normal almost immediately.

Heartworm

The most serious of the common internal parasites is the heartworm. A dog that is bitten by a mosquito infected with the heartworm *micro-filaria* (larvae) will develop worms that are 6 to 12 inches long. As these worms mature, they take up residence in the dog's heart.

The symptoms of heartworm may include coughing, tiring easily, difficulty breathing and weight loss. Heart failure and liver disease may eventually result. Verification of heartworm infection is done by drawing blood and screening for the microfilaria.

In areas where heartworm is a risk, it is best to place a dog on a preventative, usually a pill given once a month.

At least once a year a dog should have a full veterinary exami-nation. Proper care, regular vaccina-tions, periodic stool checks and

Part of maintaining your Rottweiler's health is keeping an eye out for weight problems.

preventative medications for such things as heartworm will all help ensure your dog's health.

SPAYING/ NEUTERING

Spaying a female dog or neutering a male is another way to make sure they lead long and healthy lives. Females spayed at a young age have almost no risk of developing mammary tumors or reproductive problems. Neutering a male is an excellent solution to dog aggression and also removes the chances of testicular cancer.

Female Rotties usually experience their first heat cycle somewhere between 6 months and 1 year of age. Unless spayed, they will continue to come into heat on a regular cycle. The length of time between heats varies, with anything from every six months to a year being normal.

There is absolutely no benefit to a female having a first season before being spayed, nor in letting her have a litter. The decision to breed any dog should never be taken lightly.

WHEN TO CALL THE VETERINARIAN

In any emergency situation, you should call your veterinarian immediately. You can make the difference in your dog's life by staying as calm as possible when you call and by giving the doctor or the assistant as much information as possible before you leave for the clinic. That way, the vet will be able to take immediate, specific action to remedy your dog's situation.

Emergencies include acute abdominal pain, suspected poisoning, snakebite, burns, frostbite, shock, dehydration, abnormal vomiting or bleeding and deep wounds. You are the best judge of your dog's health, as you live with and observe him every day. Don't hesitate to call your veterinarian if you suspect trouble.

The obvious considerations are whether he or she is a good physical specimen of the breed and has a sound temperament. There are several genetic problems that are common to Rotties, such as hip dysplasia, ruptured anterior cruciate ligament, entropion, cataracts and bloat. Responsible breeders screen for these prior to making breeding decisions.

Finding suitable homes for puppies is another serious consideration.

Due to their popularity, many people are attracted to Rottweilers and seek puppies without realizing the drawbacks of the breed.

Owning a dog is a lifetime commitment to that animal. There are so many unwanted dogs that people must be absolutely sure that they are not just adding to the pet overpopulation problem. When breeding a litter of puppies, it is more likely that you will lose more than you will make, when time, effort, equipment and veterinary costs are factored in.

COMMON PROBLEMS

Lameness

A limp that appears from nowhere and gets progressively worse is cause for concern. The first thing to do is try to ascertain where the problem actually is. Check the legs and feet for any areas of tenderness, swelling or infection. There are numerous possibilities to consider. In young, developing dogs, lameness in the rear can be an indication of hip dysplasia or a ruptured anterior cruciate ligament.

Hip dysplasia is a malformation of the ball and socket joint of the hips and can affect one or both sides of the dog. As a dog ages these joints wear down, and eventually arthritis is associated with the disease. Hip dysplasia can only be properly diagnosed by x-ray.

If x-rays do confirm hip dysplasia, there are several considerations. Surgery is one alternative in more serious cases. Most mildly and many moderately dysplastic dogs will lead normal lives if properly managed.

Lameness in the rear can also be a sign of a cruciate ligament problem. This ligament helps stabilize and strengthen the knee, and if it is injured over the course of time (with physical exercise) or by blunt trauma, it can rupture. A rupture causes instability, which leads to damage to the joint. Surgery can repair the damage, though the knee may never be as strong.

Not Eating or Vomiting

One of the surest signs that a Rottweiler may be ill is if he does not eat. This is why it is important to know your dog's eating habits. For most dogs, one missed meal under normal conditions is not cause for alarm, but more than that and it is time to take your dog to the veterinarian to search for reasons. The vital signs should be checked and gums examined. Normally a dog's gums are pink; if ill they will be pale and gray.

There are many reasons why dogs vomit, and many of them are not cause for alarm. If they eat too much grass they vomit. You should be concerned, however, when your dog vomits frequently over the period of a day. If the vomiting is associated with diarrhea, elevated temperature and lethargy, the cause is most likely a virus. The dog should receive supportive veterinary treatment if recovery is to proceed quickly. Vomiting that is not associated with other symptoms is often an indication of an intestinal blockage. This is often difficult for a veterinarian to diagnose, so careful monitoring is critical.

If a blockage is suspected, the first thing to do is x-ray the stomach and intestinal region. Sometimes objects will pass on their own, but usually surgical removal of the object is necessary.

Diarrhea

Diarrhea is characterized as very loose to watery stools that a

25

dog has difficulty controlling. It can be caused by anything as simple as changing diet, eating too much food, eating rich human food or having internal parasites.

First try to locate the source of the problem and remove it from the dog's access. Immediate relief is usually available by giving the dog an intestinal relief medication such as Kaopectate or Pepto-Bismol. Use the same amount per weight as for humans. Take the dog off his food for a day to allow the intestines to rest, then feed meals of cooked rice with bland ingredients added. Gradually add the dog's regular food back into his diet.

If diarrhea is bloody or has a more offensive odor than might be expected and is combined with vomiting and fever, it is most likely a virus and requires immediate veterinary attention.

Bloat

Another problem associated with the gastrointestinal system is bloat, or acute gastric dilatation. It most commonly occurs in adult dogs that eat large amounts of dry kibble. Exercise or excessive amounts of

water consumed immediately following a meal can trigger the condition.

A dog with bloat will appear restless and uncomfortable. He may drool and attempt to vomit. The abdominal area will appear swollen, and the area will be painful. In severe cases the stomach actually twists on itself and a condition called torsion occurs. If you suspect that your dog is suffering from bloat, take your dog to the nearest veterinary clinic immediately.

Bloat can be prevented by feeding smaller amounts of food several times per day rather than in one large meal. Soaking the food in water prior to feeding it will also help reduce the risk of bloat. Additionally, the dog should be kept from exercising until two or three hours after eating.

Seizures

Seizures are of the most frightening occurrences a dog owner can witness. Seizures vary in severity from trembling and stiffness to frenzied, rapid movements of the legs, foaming at the mouth and loss of urine and bowel movements. The latter is usually considered a grand mal seizure.

Seizures are caused by electrical activity in the brain, and there are many reasons why they may occur. Ingestion of some poisons, such as strychnine and insecticides, will cause seizures. These are generally long lasting and severe in nature. Injuries to the skull, tumors and cancers can trigger seizures.

If there appears to be no reason for the seizure, it is possible the cause is congenital epilepsy. This is particularly true if a dog is under the age of 3. From the age of 5, dogs are prone to develop old age onset epilepsy, which also may have a genetic predisposition.

Never try to touch or move a dog during a seizure. If there is anything nearby that might be knocked over by their flailing legs and injure them, move it out of the way. If the seizure does not stop within five minutes, call your veterinarian.

Coughing

Throughout the day most dogs will cough to get something out of their throats, and it is usually ignored. If coughing persists, then it is time to look for causes.

A common cause for a dry hacking cough is kennel cough, which is contagious and usually picked up through association with other dogs. A dog with kennel cough should receive veterinary attention and be placed on antibiotics and a cough suppressant. During treatment and recovery, the dog should be kept indoors and warm as much as possible. Kennel cough, if not cared for properly, can easily turn into pneumonia in cold conditions. Infected dogs should be isolated from other dogs until they have recovered.

Chronic coughing after exercise can also be a sign of heart failure, especially in an older dog. It may also indicate a heartworm infection. If this occurs regularly, consult your veterinarian.

Shallow breathing can be a result of an injury to the ribs or a lung

27

Applying abdominal thrusts can save a choking dog.

An Elizabethan collar keeps your dog from licking a fresh wound.

problem. A wheezing noise that can be heard as a dog breathes is an indication of a serious problem. If other symptoms include a fever and lethargy, the problem may be associated with a lung disease. The symptoms may indicate treatment for an infection. An x-ray will confirm the presence of a growth or infection in the lungs.

Skin Problems

Certain skin conditions should not be ignored if home treatment is not working. For example, if a dog is so sensitive and allergic to fleas that his coat and skin are literally destroyed by chewing, it is time to seek help. Cortisone can help relieve the itching and stop the dog from

destroying himself, but it has side effects, too! It's best to get your vet's advice.

Mange is caused by tiny mites that live on the dog's skin. The most common types are sarcoptic and demodetic mange. Diagnosis must be made by a veterinarian, because the mites are too small to be seen.

Hot spots are one of the most baffling skin problems. They can be caused by a number of things, including flea bites and allergies. A warm, moist, infected area on the skin appears out of nowhere and can be several inches large. At home one should clip the hair around it, then clean it with an antiseptic and dilute (3 percent hydrogen peroxide). Spraying with a topical anaesthetic immediately relieves itching. Topical ointments can also help. If the spot is not healing and appears to be getting larger or infected, veterinary help should be sought.

A similar type of skin condition is the lick sore. These sores are almost always on the lower part of the front legs or tops of the feet. A dog will lick a spot and out of boredom continue licking it until the hair is gone and the skin is hard, red and shiny. The sore will heal on its own if kept clean and the dog is prevented access to it by an anti-chewing spray or by wearing an Elizabethan collar.

Cuts and Wounds

Any cut over $\frac{1}{2}$ inch in length should be stitched for it to heal. Small cuts usually heal by themselves if they are rinsed well, washed with an antibiotic soap and checked regularly with further cleansing of soap or a hydrogen peroxide solution. When they occur in areas that are exposed to dirt, such as the feet, it may be advisable to place a wrap on the injury, but it should be removed frequently. If signs of infection appear, such as swelling, redness or warmth, it should be looked at by a veterinarian.

Puncture wounds should never be bandaged or stitched. They occur most commonly from bites, nails or wires. Anytime it is suspected that a dog might have been pierced by a nail or bitten, the body should be carefully examined for such wounds. As they often do not bleed very much, they can be difficult to spot. If not treated, they can result in infection or even conditions as dangerous as tetanus.

If the wound is discovered within a short time of the occurrence, try to make it bleed by applying pressure around it. Flush it with water, then clean it with soap. Leave it exposed so that oxygen is able to stay in the wound and prevent an anaerobic condition from developing. Place a dilute hydrogen peroxide on it several times a day. Watch it carefully for any indications of infection. Anytime your dog is injured, consider placing him on an antibiotic to prevent infection.

GIVING MEDICATION

When a dog has been diagnosed with a problem that requires medication it is usually in the form of a pill or liquid. Because it is essential for a dog to have the entire pill or capsule in order for the dosage to be effective, it's necessary to actually give the dog the pill rather than mix it in his food or wrap it in meat,

To give a pill, open the mouth wide, then drop it in the back of the throat.

30

which can be chewed up and spit out. Open your dog's mouth and place the pill on the back of the middle of his tongue. Then hold his head up with his mouth held shut and stroke his throat. When the dog swallows, you can let go.

Liquid medication is most easily given in a syringe. These are usually marked so the amount is accurately measured. Hold the dog's head upward at about 45°, open the mouth slightly and place the end of the syringe in the area in the back of the mouth between the cheek and rear molars. Hold your dog's mouth shut until he swallows.

If your dog needs eye medication, apply it by pulling down the lower eyelid and placing the ointment on the inside of the lid. Then

close the eye and gently disperse the solution around the eye. Eye drops can be placed directly on the eye. Giving ear medicine is similar to cleaning the ears. The drops are placed in the canal and the ear is then massaged.

COMMON ROTTWEILER PROBLEMS

CATARACTS—There are several types of cataracts that affect Rotties. They are characterized by the part of the lens on which they appear and the age of the dog. Most are genetic, though others can be caused by injury or the aging process. Most cataracts are nonprogressive in Rottweilers and impairment of vision is usually mild. Diagnosis must be made by a veterinary ophthalmologist.

LOW THYROID (HYPOTHYROIDISM)— It may be genetic and is also associated with poor immunity. There may be physical signs, such as weight gain, lethargy, poor coat, infertility in both sexes and longer than normal periods of time between heat

Squeeze eye ointment into the lower lid.

Use a scarf to make a temporary muzzle, as shown.

cycles. A thyroid test will indicate if there is a problem. Daily medication will correct the thyroid levels and return a dog to normal.

PROGRESSIVE RETINAL ATROPHY (PRA)—This is less common in Rottweilers than cataracts, but it still occurs. PRA is a gradual degeneration of the cells of the retina. It first occurs in middle-aged dogs and leads to loss of vision. Diagnosis is the same as for cataracts.

SUBAORTIC STENOSIS (SAS)—This is a genetically caused defect that is detected by a murmur, and accurate diagnosis is made by a variety of advanced techniques including auscultation and echocardiogram. In cases of minor murmurs, a dog should lead a normal, though sedate, life. Dogs with severe grades of SAS will show physical signs and often die unexpectedly

at a young age. Diagnosis should be made by a registered canine cardiologist.

VON WILLEBRANDS DISEASE—This is a genetic bleeding disorder that might be suspected if it takes longer than normal for a wound to stop bleeding. Other indications are high mortality rates in newborn puppies or poor fertility in a female. A blood specimen treated and tested at a specially equipped facility is necessary to diagnose this disease.

FIRST AID AND EMERGENCIES

First-aid measures can be taken to help ensure that your dog gets to a veterinarian in time for treatment to be effective.

Anytime a dog is in extreme pain, even the most docile one may bite if touched. As a precaution, the dog's mouth should be restrained with some type of muzzle. A rope, pair of pantyhose or strip of cloth

IDENTIFYING YOUR DOG

It's a terrible thing to think about, but your dog could somehow, someday, get lost or stolen. How would you get him back? Your best bet would be to have some form of identification on your dog. You can choose from a collar and tags, a tattoo, a microchip or a combination of these three.

Every dog should wear a buckle collar with identification tags. They are the quickest and easiest way for a stranger to identify your dog. It's best to inscribe the tags with your name and phone number; you don't need to include your dog's name.

There are two ways to permanently identify your dog. The first is a tattoo, placed on the inside of your dog's thigh. The tattoo should be your social security number or your dog's AKC registration number.

The second is a microchip, a rice-grain-sized pellet that's inserted under the dog's skin at the base of the neck, between the shoulder blades. When a scanner is passed over the dog, it will beep, notifying the person that the dog has a chip. The scanner will then show a code, identifying the dog. Microchips are becoming more and more popular and are certainly the wave of the future.

about 2 feet long all work in a pinch.

First tie a loose knot that has an opening large enough to easily fit around the dog's nose. Once it is on, tighten the knot on the top of the muzzle. Then bring the two ends down and tie another knot underneath the dog's chin. Finally, pull the ends behind the head and tie a knot below the ears. Don't do this if there is an injury to the head or the dog requires artificial respiration.

If a dog has been injured or is too ill to walk on his own, he will have to carried to be moved. It is important to be very careful when this is done to prevent further injury or trauma. Keep the dog's body as flat and still as possible. Two people are usually needed to move a large dog. A blanket can work if all four corners are held taut. A piece of plywood or extremely stiff cardboard works best, if available.

ARTIFICIAL RESPIRATION—

Artificial respiration is necessary if breathing has stopped. Situations that may cause a state of unconsciousness include drowning, choking, electric shock or even shock itself. If you've taken a course in human CPR, you will discover that similar methods are used on dogs. The first thing to do is check the mouth and air passages for any object that might obstruct breathing. If you find nothing, or when it is cleared, hold the dog's mouth while covering the nose completely with your mouth. Gently exhale into the dog's nose. This should be done at between ten to twelve breaths per minute.

If the heart has stopped beating, place the dog on his right side and place the palm of your hand on the rib cage just behind the elbows. Press down six times and then wait five seconds and repeat. This should be done in conjunction with artificial respiration, so it will require two people. Artificial respiration should be continued until the dog breathes on his own or the heart beats. Heart massage should continue until the heart beats on its own or no beat is felt for five minutes.

SHOCK—Whenever a dog is injured or is seriously ill, the odds are good that he will go into a state of shock. A dog in shock will be listless, weak and cold to the touch. His gums will be pale. If not treated, a dog will die from shock, even if the illness or

Keeping your dog on a leash while outside can help to protect your Rottweiler from all types of dangers.

33

injuries themselves are not fatal. The conditions of the dog should continue to be treated, but the dog should be kept as comfortable as possible. A blanket can help keep the dog warm. A dog in shock needs immediate veterinary care.

SEVERE BLEEDING—When severe bleeding from a cut occurs, the area should be covered with bandaging material or a clean cloth and should have pressure applied to it. If it appears that an artery is involved and the wound is on a limb, then a

Some of the many household substances harmful to your dog.

tourniquet should be applied. This can be made of a piece of cloth, gauze or sock if nothing else is available. It should be tied above the wound and checked every few minutes to make sure it is not so tight that circulation to the rest of the limb is cut off.

FRACTURE—If a fracture is felt or suspected, the dog should be moved

A healthy Rottweiler will have bright, shiny eyes and a shiny coat.

and transported as carefully as possible to a veterinarian. Attempting to treat a break at home can cause more damage than leaving it alone.

POISONING—In the case of poisoning the only thing to do is get help immediately. If you know the source of the poison, take the container or object with you, as this may aid treatment.

In acidic or alkaline poisonings the chemicals must be neutralized. Pepto-Bismol or milk of magnesia at 2 teaspoons per 5 pounds of weight can be given for acids. Vinegar diluted at one part to four parts water at the same dosage can relieve alkaline poisons.

HEATSTROKE—Heatstroke occurs when a dog's body temperature greatly exceeds the normal 101.5°F. It can be caused by overexercise in warm temperatures or if a dog is left in a closed vehicle for any period of time. A dog should *never* be left in an unventilated, unshaded vehicle. Even if you only plan to be gone for a minute, that time can unexpectedly increase and place a dog in a life-threatening situation.

34

Dogs suffering from heatstroke will feel hot to the touch and inhale short, shallow, rapid breaths. The heartbeat will be very fast. The dog must be cooled immediately, preferably being wet down with cool water in any way that is available. The dog should be wrapped in cool, damp towels.

The opposite of heatstroke is hypothermia. When a dog is exposed to extreme cold for long periods of time, his body temperature drops, he becomes chilled and he can go into shock. The dog should be placed in a warm environment and wrapped in towels or blankets. If the dog is already wet, a warm bath can help. Massaging the body will help increase the circulation to normal levels.

INSECT BITES—The seriousness of reactions to insect bites varies. The affected area will be red, swollen and painful. In the case of bee stings the stinger should always be removed. A paste made of baking soda and water can be applied to the wound and ice applied to the area for the relief of swelling. The bites of some spiders, centipedes and scorpions can cause severe illness and lead to shock.

A FIRST-AID KIT

Keep a canine first-aid kit on hand for general care and emergencies. Check it periodically to make sure liquids haven't spilled or dried up, and replace medications and materials after they're used. Your kit should include:

- Activated charcoal tablets
- Adhesive tape (1 and 2 inches wide)
- Antibacterial ointment (for skin and eyes)
- Aspirin (buffered or enteric coated, *not* Ibuprofen)
- Bandages: gauze rolls (1 and 2 inches wide) and dressing pads
- Cotton balls
- Diarrhea medicine
- Dosing syringe
- Hydrogen peroxide (3%)
- Petroleum jelly
- Rectal thermometer
- Rubber gloves
- Rubbing alcohol
- Scissors
- Tourniquet
- Towel
- Tweezers

35

CHAPTER FOUR

Positively Nutritious

The nutritional needs of a dog will change throughout her life-time. It is necessary to be aware of these changes not only for proper initial growth to occur, but also so your dog can lead a healthy life for many years.

When a puppy first leaves the home of her breeder, she should have been weaned from her dam for at least one week and should be eating puppy food. Be sure to ask what type of puppy food that is and plan on continuing to use it for at least the first few days your puppy is in her new home. If it's a premium dog food and is readily available where you live, there is no reason not to continue feeding it. If for some reason you wish to switch food, then do so gradually. Ask the breeder to give you several days' supply, and

gradually mix it in with the new food.

TYPES OF DOG FOODS

Dog foods are available in several forms—dry (kibble), canned or semimoist. Kibble is the preferred form not only because of economy or ease of preparation, but also because the other forms do not meet the dietary needs of the Rottweiler.

Canned foods are not recommended for a Rottweiler. If you are feeding a good-quality kibble and preparing it properly, there is no need to add canned food (or anything else) to induce the dog to eat. A healthy dog with adequate exercise who has not been taught bad eating habits will devour food. A well-balanced, completely nutritious dry kibble, free of artificial preservatives, is the preferred choice of most knowledgeable dog owners.

FEEDING YOUR PUPPY

If you're feeding a puppy (under 6 months of age), select one of the

HOW TO READ THE DOG-FOOD LABEL

With so many choices on the market, how can you be sure you are feeding the right food for your dog? The information is all there on the label—if you know what you're looking for.

Look for the nutritional claim right up top. Is the food "100% nutritionally complete"? If so, it's for nearly all life stages; "growth and maintenance," on the other hand, is for early development; puppy foods are marked as such, as are foods for senior dogs.

Ingredients are listed in descending order by weight. The first three or four ingredients will tell you the bulk of what the food contains. Look for the highest-quality ingredients, like meats and grains, to be among them.

The guaranteed analysis tells you what levels of protein, fat, fiber and moisture are in the food, in that order. While these numbers are meaningful, they won't tell you much about the quality of the food. Nutritional value is in the dry matter, not the moisture content.

In many ways, seeing is believing. If your dog has bright eyes, a shiny coat, a good appetite and a good energy level, chances are her diet's fine. Your dog's breeder and your veterinarian are good sources of advice if you're still confused.

It's best to feed your puppy a food specially formulated for the needs of a young dog.

daily. The rate of growth in a breed like the Rottweiler is tremendous, from possibly $3/4$ pound at birth to possibly 100 pounds at one year. Puppies need a food that meets the demands of their bodies but does not encourage or promote excessive early growth. For this reason, at approximately 5 months of age, you may start switching the puppies to an adult formula and by 6 months the transition is complete.

A healthy Rottweiler, puppy or adult, should be an eager eater. Puppies lose their concentration easily, so it's best to feed them in a restricted space. If the dog has not cleaned up the food in a

quality foods formulated specifically for puppies. Puppies need to be fed small amounts, three or four times

Most experts recommend a consistent feeding schedule that avoids letting a dog be a "self-feeder."

reasonable amount of time (roughly fifteen minutes), remove the pan and refrigerate the food until the next scheduled feeding. If poor appetite persists, visit your veterinarian.

FEEDING YOUR ADULT

Adult dogs need an adult maintenance diet, based on normal activity. There are some who feel that feeding two meals per day decreases bloat. Intake can vary from dog to dog, depending on activity level and how much time she spends outside. Older dogs have lower caloric requirements; if the dog is really a dedicated eater, it is better to feed the usual amount of a food lower in calories than to simply reduce the amount of a higher calorie food.

The recommended amount for the average Rottweiler is 3 to 4 cups. However, the amount of food an adult Rottweiler should eat daily will vary according to the size of the dog and her activity level. The physical appearance a Rottweiler presents is as much a result of genetics as the food she eats. The owner that feeds a high quality food

TYPES OF FOODS/TREATS

There are three types of commercially available dog food—dry, canned and semimoist —and a huge assortment of treats (lucky dogs!) to feed your dog. Which should you choose?

Dry and canned foods contain similar ingredients. The primary difference between them is their moisture content. The moisture is not just water. It's blood and broth, too, the very things that dogs adore. So while canned food is more palatable, dry food is more economical, convenient and effective in controlling tartar buildup. Most owners feed a 25 percent canned/75 percent dry diet to give their dogs the benefit of both. Just be sure your dog is getting the nutrition she needs (you and your veterinarian can determine this).

Semimoist foods have the flavor dogs love and the convenience owners want. However, they tend to contain excessive amounts of artificial colors and preservatives.

Dog treats come in every size, shape and flavor imaginable, from organic cookies shaped like postal carriers to beefy chew sticks. Dogs seem to love them all, so enjoy the variety. Just be sure not to overindulge your dog. Factor treats into her regular meal sizes.

and keeps her at optimum weight will be rewarded with a healthy and fit Rottweiler.

How Many Meals a Day?

Individual dogs vary in how much they should eat to maintain a desired body weight—not too fat, but not too thin. Puppies need several meals a day, while older dogs may need only one. Determine how much food keeps your adult dog looking and feeling her best. Then decide how many meals you want to feed with that amount. Like us, most dogs love to eat, and offering two meals a day is more enjoyable for them. If you're worried about overfeeding, make sure you measure correctly and abstain from adding tidbits to the meals.

Whether you feed one or two meals, only leave your dog's food out for the amount of time it takes her to eat it—ten minutes, for example. Free-feeding (when food is available anytime) and leisurely meals encourage picky eating. Don't worry if your dog doesn't finish all her dinner in the allotted time. She'll learn she should.

Adding Extras

Whether or not to feed table scraps is controversial. If you add scraps to your dog's diet, make certain that this does not include chocolate, pastry, candy, potatoes, onions, greasy food and so forth. Table scraps should never constitute more than 25 percent of the dog's diet at any given meal. If you indulge your Rottweiler with meat scraps from dinner, be certain to remove the fat.

Vegetables and Fruit

Some vegetables are relished by dogs (tomatoes, for example) and, in moderation, can have very beneficial effects. Others (like cabbage) are indigestible and may cause flatulence. Many Rottweilers thoroughly enjoy fruit—grapes, bananas and so forth; however, be very wary of fruits containing pits, especially apricots, peaches and cherries. The pits of these fruits contain cyanide. Even pits that don't contain any toxin should be kept from the dog because they can cause blockage.

Meat Treats and Bones

It's not necessary to add meat to a well-balanced kibble, but if you insist on doing so, the meat should be cooked, never fed raw. Dogs should not have any real bone except a big beef knuckle bone, and the

only purpose this serves is for
personal enjoyment and polishing
the teeth.

FOODS TO AVOID

Spicy foods (like pizza or chili) play
havoc with the Rottweiler's digestive
system. Dogs cannot assimilate the
raw egg white. Never feed a whole
cooked egg—it may lodge in the
dog's windpipe. Avoid commercial
canine food enhancers. They con-
sist of artificial colors and flavors
and water. A normal, healthy
Rottweiler should not have to be
coaxed or duped into eating palatable food.

Never, ever give your dog chocolate. Chocolate contains a substance
called theobromine, which is highly
toxic to dogs. Ingestion of even a
small amount may prove fatal. Dogs
don't need variety in their diet or to
learn to beg for food, either from
your hand or the table. The opposite
is true. Find a quality kibble that
your dog thrives on, and if you are
wise, never introduce your dog to
people food.

*While nursing,
puppies get all
the nutrients
they need from
their mom. But
after that, it's
up to you to
provide the best
food for them.*

41

CHAPTER FIVE

Putting on the Dog

There is an old saying among breeders that a good coat is "bred for, fed for and cared for." As with most old sayings, there's a good deal of truth in it. Whether or not a good coat was part of your Rottweiler's inheritance is beyond your control. However, you can do your best with what you have. The number one rule is that the coat must look and feel clean and smell pleasant.

GIVING YOUR ROTTWEILER A BATH

The bath: Most dogs with undercoats such as the Rottweiler's do not require frequent bathing. Generally, spring and autumn baths are sufficient unless the dog has rolled in something offensive or has gotten something on his coat that must be removed.

Very young puppies should not be bathed. Puppies aged 12 weeks or older, when bathed, should be kept in a very warm room until the coat is thoroughly dry.

Make certain that towels and shampoo designed for dogs are handy before starting, so you never have a reason to leave the tub while the dog is in it. Before getting the animal wet, plug his ears with wads of cotton and place a drop of mineral oil in each eye to prevent soap burn. Use a spray nozzle to wet the dog, then lather and rinse the head, being careful to keep soap and water out of eyes and ears. After the head has been thoroughly rinsed, shampoo the rest of the dog. Rinsing is of critical importance; if any shampoo residue is left, it can seriously irritate the skin and dull the coat. Towel the dog vigorously, removing as much water as possible.

In very warm weather, an adult dog may be left outside to dry. If there's a chill in the air, bring an adult dog indoors. Even inside a warm house, the dog may chill

Your dog may not like it much, but an occasional bath is important.

43

because his coat is wet. It helps if you teach your dog to submit to a blow dryer. It should always be kept on a low setting.

If you have a hot water pipe installed to an outside faucet, you

GROOMING TOOLS

pin brush	scissors
slicker brush	nail clippers
flea comb	tooth-cleaning equipment
towel	shampoo
matt rake	conditioner
grooming mitt	clippers

can mix hot and cold water to a suitable temperature (hot enough to feel comfortable to your hand) and use the garden hose to bathe your dog in good weather.

REGULAR BRUSHING

Nothing beats regular brushing for keeping a coat in good condition; it also provides a wonderful opportunity to examine your dog for abnormal lesions, lumps, sore spots and so forth as well as giving you the chance to use obedience commands in a practical circumstance. A grooming mitt (i.e., a mitt that fits

over your hand and is smooth on one side, with soft wire pins on the other) is ideal for a Rottweiler. Brushing should be a daily activity and is one that most dogs enjoy. After all, the dog is getting your undivided attention.

During the spring, when the Rottweiler loses his undercoat, you may have to use several tools—brushes, combs and so forth.

TAKING CARE OF TOENAILS

Trimming nails is essential for the well-being of your dog's feet. Dogs that receive lots of exercise or that are on cement may wear their nails down enough on their own that clipping is unnecessary. But even these dogs, as they become older and less active, will need nail care. Normally, nails should be trimmed every two weeks or when the nails start to touch the floor. This is noticeable as a clicking sound when the dog walks on hard surfaces.

Puppies may be started off with a guillotine-type nail clipper, removing just the pointed tip. If you cut too much, you will cut the quick—the sensitive part containing nerves and blood vessels—causing pain and

A grooming mitt is an ideal tool for daily coat maintenance.

bleeding. A styptic powder will help to stop the bleeding; if it doesn't, applying the powder along with some pressure does the job.

If clipping nails is a scary proposition for you, most groomers and veterinary clinics will take care of it for a small fee.

ABOUT EARS

Ears should be wiped out once a week with a wad of soft cotton. It's not necessary to put anything on the cotton. Examine the eyes and ears after the dog has had a run in tall grass; remove any seeds or foreign matter.

FOR ALL-OVER GOOD HEALTH

Probably because no one ever told them about the importance of regular inspection, most pet owners seldom get past the top of the head. However, to keep your dog in good health and catch problems before they become serious, make it a point to examine teeth, inside the mouth, under the tongue, eyes, ears, paws, under-carriage, penile sheath and testicles of the male, vulva of the female and area surrounding

A shedding blade will come in handy during the spring, when your Rottweiler's undercoat begins to shed.

45

The most important thing to remember when clipping your dog's toenails is to avoid cutting into the quick.

the anus. This inspection can be incorporated into your routine grooming.

CHAPTER SIX

Measuring Up

Any definition of the Rottweiler would be incomplete without an explanation of the official standard of the breed. Each standard is prepared by the national breed club and approved by the American Kennel Club (AKC), the principal registry of purebred dogs in the United States. The standard provides a physical description of the breed with limited reference to temperament. It is important to keep in mind when reading the standard and trying to match one's own Rottweiler to it that the standard describes an *ideal* Rottweiler.

What follows is the official standard for the Rottweiler. An explanation of the standard is given later in the chapter.

General Appearance

The ideal Rottweiler is a medium large, robust and powerful dog, black with clearly defined rust markings. His compact and substantial build denotes great strength, agility and endurance. Dogs are characteristically more massive throughout with larger frame and heavier bone than bitches. Bitches are distinctly feminine but without weakness of substance or structure.

Size, Proportion, Substance Dogs

24 inches to 27 inches. Bitches—22 inches to 25 inches, with preferred size being mid-range of each sex. Correct proportion is of primary importance, as long as size is within the standard's range. The length of body, from prosternum to the rearmost projection of the rump, is slightly longer than the height of the dog at the withers, the most desirable proportion of the height to length being 9 to 10. The Rottweiler is neither coarse nor shelly. Depth of chest is approximately fifty percent (50%) of the height of the dog. His bone and muscle mass must be sufficient to balance his frame, giving a

WHAT IS A BREED STANDARD?

A breed standard—a detailed description of an individual breed—is meant to portray the ideal specimen of that breed. Because the standard describes an ideal specimen, it isn't based on any particular dog. It is a concept against which judges compare actual dogs and breeders strive to produce dogs.

compact and very powerful appearance. Serious Faults—Lack of proportion, undersized, oversized, reversal of sex characteristics (bitchy dogs, doggy bitches).

Head

Of medium length, broad between the ears; forehead line seen in profile is moderately arched; zygomatic arch and stop well developed with strong broad upper and lower jaws. The desired ratio of backskull to muzzle is 3 to 2. Forehead is preferred dry, however some wrinkling may occur when dog is alert. *Expression* is noble, alert, and self-assured. *Eyes* of medium size, almond shaped with well fitting lids, moderately deep-set, neither protruding nor receding. The desired color is a uniform dark brown. Serious Faults—Yellow (bird of prey) eyes, eyes of different color or size, hairless eye rim. Disqualifications—Entropion, Ectropion. *Ears* of medium size, pendant, triangular in shape; when carried alertly the ears are level with the top of the skull and appear to broaden it. Ears are to be set well apart, hanging forward with the inner edge lying tightly against the head and terminating at approximately mid-cheek.

A Rottweiler's expression should be noble and self-assured.

Serious Faults—Improper carriage (creased, folded or held away from cheek/head). *Muzzle*—Bridge is straight, broad at base with slight tapering towards tip. The end of the muzzle is broad with well developed chin. *Nose* is broad rather than round and always black. *Lips*—Always black; corners closed; inner mouth pigment is preferred dark. Serious Faults—Total lack of mouth pigment (pink mouth). *Bite and Dentition*—Teeth 42 in number (20 upper, 22 lower), strong, correctly placed, meeting in a scissors bite—lower incisors touching inside of upper incisors. Serious Faults—Level bite; any missing tooth. Disqualifications—Overshot, undershot (when incisors do not touch or mesh); wry mouth; two or more missing teeth.

Neck, Topline, Body

Neck—Powerful, well muscled, moderately long, slightly arched and without loose skin. *Topline*—The back is firm and level, extending in a straight line from behind the withers to the croup. The back remains horizontal to the ground while the dog is moving or standing. *Body*—The chest is roomy, broad and deep, reaching to elbow, with well pronounced forechest and well sprung, oval ribs. Back is straight and strong. Loin is short, deep and well muscled. Croup is broad, of medium length and only slightly sloping. Underline of a mature Rottweiler has a slight tuck-up. Males must have two normal testicles properly descended into the scrotum. Disqualifications—Unilateral cryptorchid or cryptorchid males. *Tail*—Tail docked short, close to body, leaving one or two tail vertebrae. The set of the tail is more important than length. Properly set, it gives an impression of elongation of topline; carried slightly above horizontal when the dog is excited or moving.

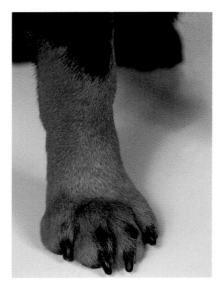

A Rottweiler's feet are round and compact, with short, black nails.

shoulder blade, set so elbows are well under body. Distance from withers to elbow and elbow to ground is equal. Legs are strongly developed with straight, heavy bone, not set close together. Pasterns are strong, springy and almost perpendicular to the ground. Feet are round, compact with well arched toes, turning neither in nor out. Pads are thick and hard. Nails short, strong and black. Dewclaws may be removed.

Forequarters

Shoulder blade is long and well laid back. Upper arm equal in length to

Hindquarters

Angulation of hindquarters balances that of forequarters. Upper thigh is

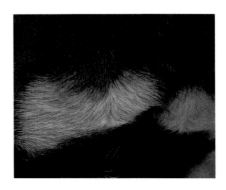

A Rottweiler's coat is dense, and is always black with rust to mahogany markings.

fairly long, very broad and well muscled. Stifle joint is well turned. Lower thigh is long, broad and powerful, with extensive muscling leading into a strong hock joint. Rear pasterns are nearly perpendicular to the ground. Viewed from the rear, hind legs are straight, strong and wide enough apart to fit with a properly built body. Feet are somewhat longer than the front feet, turning neither in nor out, equally compact with well arched toes. Pads are thick and hard. Nails short, strong, and black. Dewclaws must be removed.

Coat

Outer coat is straight, coarse, dense, of medium length and lying flat. Undercoat should be present on neck and thighs, but the amount is influenced by climatic conditions. Undercoat should not show through outer coat. The coat is shortest on head, ears and legs, longest on breeching. The Rottweiler is to be exhibited in the natural condition with no trimming. Fault—Wavy coat. Serious Faults—Open, excessively short, or curly coat; total lack of undercoat; any trimming that alters the length of the natural coat. Disqualifications—Long coat.

Color

Always black with rust to mahogany markings. The demarcation between black and rust is to be clearly defined. The markings should be located as follows: a spot over each eye; on cheeks; as a strip around each side of muzzle, but not on the bridge of nose; on throat; triangular mark on both sides of prosternum; on forelegs from carpus downward to the toes; on inside of rear legs showing down the front of the stifle and broadening out to front of rear legs from hock to toes but not completely eliminating black from rear of pasterns; under tail; black penciling on toes. The undercoat is gray, tan, or black. Quantity and location of rust markings is important and should not exceed ten percent of body color. Serious Faults—Straw colored, excessive, insufficient or sooty markings; rust marking other than described above; white marking any place on dog (a few rust or white hairs do not constitute a marking). Disqualifications—Any base color other than black; absence of all markings.

Gait

The Rottweiler is a trotter. His movement should be balanced, harmonious, sure, powerful and unhindered, with strong forereach and a powerful rear drive. The motion is effortless, efficient, and ground covering. Front and rear legs are thrown neither in nor out, as the imprint of hind feet should touch that of forefeet. In a trot the forequarters and hindquarters are mutually coordinated while the back remains level, firm and relatively motionless. As speed increases the legs will converge under body towards a center line.

Temperament

The Rottweiler is basically a calm, confident and courageous dog with a self-assured aloofness that does not lend itself to immediate and indiscriminate friendships. A Rottweiler is self-confident and responds quietly and with a wait-and-see attitude to influences in his environment. He has an inherent desire to protect home and family, and is an intelligent dog of extreme hardness and adaptability with a strong willingness to work, making him especially suited as a companion, guardian and general all-purpose dog. The behavior of the Rottweiler in the show ring should be controlled, willing and adaptable, trained to submit to examination of

Even as puppies, Rottweilers show their potential to be strong and sturdy working dogs.

mouth, testicles, etc. An aloof or reserved dog should not be penalized as this reflects the accepted character of the breed. An aggressive or belligerent attitude towards other dogs should not be faulted. A judge shall excuse from the ring any shy Rottweiler. A dog shall be judged fundamentally shy if, refusing to stand for examination, he shrinks away from the judge. A dog that in the opinion of the judge menaces or threatens him/her, or exhibits any sign that he may not be safely approached or examined by the judge in the normal manner, shall be excused from the ring. A dog that in the opinion of the judge attacks any person in the ring shall be disqualified.

Summary

The foregoing is a description of the ideal Rottweiler. Any structural fault that detracts from the above described working dog must be penalized to the extent of the deviation.

Disqualifications

Entropion, ectropion. Overshot, undershot (when incisors do not touch or mesh); wry mouth: two or more missing teeth. Unilateral cryptorchid or cryptorchid males. Long coat. Any base color other than black; absence of all markings. A dog that in the opinion of the judge attacks any person in the ring.

ANOTHER LOOK AT THE STANDARD

How important is the standard to you in selecting your Rottweiler? It can be of great value if you understand that the standard represents an ideal but that few things in life come close to being ideal.

Size, Proportion, Substance

First and foremost, the Rottweiler is a working dog. If too large, the dog is usually too clumsy and awkward; if too small, the dog lacks the strength and power to do the work she was bred for.

Head

EYES
Hairless eye rim can be a serious health problem. The skin may grow

coarse, puffy or itchy, causing the dog to paw at it or rub it against furniture or carpet. This may abrade the skin or injure the eye. Entropion (where the eyelid turns inward) and ectropion (where the eyelid rolls away from the eye) are serious flaws. Both can only be corrected surgically.

BITE AND DENTITION

A Rottweiler with a level bite or one that is overshot or undershot is still an excellent candidate for the pet owner. However, dogs with wry mouth (where jaws do not align) or grossly overshot or undershot bites may have serious problems with eating. Form follows function.

Coat

There is no room for personal preference. Rottweilers are black with rust to mahogany markings. There is no genetic reason for Rottweilers to have a base coat other than black. Total absence of markings may indicate questionable ancestry.

Temperament

It cannot be said often enough that the Rottweiler was bred to work.

Not only is the dog extremely quick to learn the things her owner teaches, but also she has a remarkable ability to figure out things without benefit of instruction. This dog, for many years, went about her job as drover, guardian, police dog or military dog with a minimum of fuss.

No one can or should choose to ignore bad temperament. Due to the breed's popularity, breeding has increased—the gene pool expanded so greatly and so randomly that there is now a wide range of temperaments to be found.

THE AMERICAN KENNEL CLUB

Familiarly referred to as "the AKC," the American Kennel Club is a nonprofit organization devoted to the advancement of purebred dogs. The AKC maintains a registry of recognized breeds and adopts and enforces rules for dog events including shows, obedience trials and the Canine Good Citizen program. It is a club of clubs, established in 1884 and composed, today, of over 500 autonomous dog clubs throughout the United States. Each club is represented by a delegate; the delegates make up the legislative body of the AKC, voting on rules and electing directors.

CHAPTER SEVEN

A Matter of Fact

the journey required using many dogs to act as drovers and guard dogs for the herds. These dogs were of no particular breed, but in general resembled the Mastiff; they were large and powerful, courageous and steadfast—a formidable force.

Many Romans settled on the banks of the Neckar River, whose climate and soil combined to provide an ideal place for raising cattle. It can only be assumed that during the next few hundred years, descendants of the dogs that crossed the Alps with the Romans continued their role as guardian and drover's dog. The settlement flourished and became a major trade and cattle center. Butchers were an important

History tells us that when the Romans invaded Europe, they did so with vast armies, which required vast supplies of food. Much of this food was beef on the hoof, so

Rottweilers have a long history as herding dogs.

part of the community, and their dogs were known as *Metzgerhunds* (butcher dogs).

RED TILE TOWN DOGS

Because of the red-tiled roofing on some of the original Roman buildings, the town became known as Rote Wil (Red Tile). Eventually, it was called Rottweil, and the work-

ing cattle dogs from there were called Rottweilers. Other than the nobility or aristocracy, people in those days would not or could not afford to feed any animal that did not earn his keep. The larger dogs were used by the butchers to drive cattle as well as to guard them in the pens before butchering. It is said that smaller specimens of this breed that had derived from the Roman dogs were used for more domestic work at the butcher's home.

Finding a New Job

About the middle of the nineteenth century, a law was passed forbidding the driving of cattle over roads; almost simultaneously, the railroad and the donkey replaced the Rottweiler as a cart dog. A few years before World War I, only one Rottweiler bitch existed in the town of Rottweil. In 1901, efforts were made to form a Rottweiler (and Leonberger) Club. The club did not last long but can take credit for producing the first Rottweiler standard.

The work ethic was implanted in the Rottweiler during his develop-ment in Germany. The farmers and butchers cared little for aesthetic appearance in a dog; if a good working bitch came in season and a good working male was available, a breeding sometimes took place. If the dog didn't work, he didn't survive. "A good working dog is eager to work and is the worse for not being used."

THE ROTTWEILER IN THE U.S.

Rottweilers were imported into this country by their German owners who emigrated here and by Americans who had visited Germany and had been impressed by the Rottweiler. In 1931, the first Rottweiler was listed in the AKC Stud Book, and for a time the breed enjoyed a slow increase in popular-ity. After World War II, however, returning servicemen who had been stationed in Germany and had seen this breed do its work in the mili-tary, railroad yards and so forth were quick to try to import animals for their own use. They were not so much interested in show or breeding stock but wanted dogs that would *work*! Many of these men naturally gravitated from the military into law enforcement or private security.

A Rottweiler's instinctive territorial nature makes him an effective guard dog.

By this time, it had become the in thing to own a purebred dog registered with the AKC. It neither mattered whether he was a correct representative of the breed nor what kind of temperament or needs the dog had. The rarer the breed, the higher the status of the owner. Having little or no knowledge of canine genetics and even less insight into proper rearing and training of such a determined animal as the Rottweiler, these owners embarked on a course that could only be detrimental to the breed.

THE RISE—AND FALL—OF THE ROTTWEILER

While knowledgeable and ethical breeders pored over pedigrees, looking for the right stud dog for their bitch, while they x-rayed hips and elbows to determine that their breeding stock was free from genetic skeletal problems, while they carefully evaluated temperament in their dogs, Fred and Ethel merrily bred any dog to any bitch, neglecting to do any screening of breeding stock or potential puppy buyers. Coincidentally, the crime rate in America started a sharp upswing,

WHERE DID DOGS COME FROM?

It can be argued that dogs were right there at man's side from the beginning of time. As soon as human beings began to document their existence, the dog was among their drawings and inscriptions. Dogs were not just friends, they served a purpose: There were dogs to hunt birds, pull sleds, herd sheep, burrow after rats—even sit in laps! What your dog was originally bred to do influences the way he behaves. The American Kennel Club recognizes over 140 breeds, and there are hundreds more distinct breeds around the world. To make sense of the breeds, they are grouped according to their size or function. The AKC has seven groups:

1. Sporting
2. Working
3. Herding
4. Hounds
5. Terriers
6. Toys
7. Non-Sporting

Can you name a breed from each group? Here's some help: (1) Golden Retriever; (2) Doberman Pinscher; (3) Collie; (4) Beagle; (5) Scottish Terrier; (6) Maltese; and (7) Dalmatian. All modern domestic dogs (*Canis familiaris*) are related, however different they look, and are all descended from *Canis lupus*, the gray wolf. The Rottweiler was— and is—a drover and herder.

57

The Rottweiler is one of the most popular breeds used for guard dog duty, but serious policing is still best left to the professionals.

ship" as much as the Rottweiler has. Everyone from rock stars to entire football teams have been Rottweiler owners. Irresponsible training has, at times, led to tragic consequences, causing the Rottweiler to be pegged as a "killer dog." People outside the law have purchased Rottweilers for their own nefarious purposes—to guard their marijuana plantations, to guard their stash of cocaine, to guard their illegal weapons and also to participate in that reprehensible activity—pitting dogs against each other in fights to the death.

LOVED FOR THE RIGHT REASONS

Fortunately, the majority of Rottweiler owners love, understand and respect the breed. Rottweilers have become widely recognized for their excellent work as therapy dogs; their owners visit hospitals and nursing homes, and the dogs are trained to be gentle "angels of mercy."

The Rottweiler continues to enjoy prestige as a versatile dog for law enforcement; in addition, a keen sense of smell and dedication to duty make the dog frequently the

and suddenly people felt that they had to have a "guard dog."

Probably no recognized breed has suffered from "celebrity owner-

FAMOUS OWNERS OF ROTTWEILERS

Shannon Doherty	Christian Slater
John Larroquette	Randy White
Barry Larkin	Stevie Wonder
Jack Scalia	

breed of choice for many search and rescue groups. Recently, the AKC acknowledged the Rottweiler's ability as a herder by permitting the breed to compete in AKC-sanctioned herding trials.

In short, Rottweilers enjoy most activities involving their owners and physical energy because the breed was genetically engineered to be physically, mentally and emotionally active.

With love, respect and training from their owners, Rottweilers become great family pets.

59

CHAPTER EIGHT

On Good Behavior

by Ian Dunbar, Ph.D., MRCVS

Training is the jewel in the crown—the most important aspect of doggy husbandry. There is no more important variable influencing dog behavior and temperament than the dog's education: A well-trained, well-behaved and good-natured puppydog is always a joy to live with, but an untrained and uncivilized dog can be a perpetual nightmare. Moreover, deny the dog an education and she will not have the opportunity to fulfill her own canine potential; neither will she have the ability to communicate effectively with her human companions.

Luckily, modern psychological training methods are easy, efficient, effective and, above all, considerably dog-friendly and user-friendly. Doggy education is as simple as it is enjoyable. But before you can have a good time play-training with your new dog, you have to learn what to do and how to do it. There is no bigger variable influencing the success of dog training than the owner's experience and expertise. Before you embark on the dog's education, you must first educate yourself.

BASIC TRAINING FOR OWNERS

Ideally, basic owner training should begin well before you select your dog. Find out all you can about your chosen breed first, then master rudimentary training and handling skills. If you already have your puppydog, owner training is a dire emergency —the clock is ticking! Especially for puppies, the first few weeks at home are the most important and influential days in the dog's life. Indeed, the cause of most adolescent and adult problems may be traced back to the initial days the pup explores her new home. This is the time to establish the *status quo*—to teach the puppydog how you would like her to behave and so prevent otherwise quite predictable problems.

In addition to consulting breeders and breed books such as this one (which understandably have a positive breed bias), seek out as many pet owners with your breed as you can find. Good points are obvious. What you want to find out are the breed-specific problems, so you can nip them in the bud. In particular, you should talk to owners with adolescent dogs and make a list of all anticipated problems. Most important, test drive at least half a dozen adolescent and adult dogs of your breed yourself. An 8-week-old puppy is deceptively easy to handle, but she will acquire adult size, speed and strength in just four months, so you should learn now what to prepare for.

Puppy and pet dog training classes offer a convenient venue to locate pet owners and observe dogs in action. For a list of suitable trainers in your area, contact the Association of Pet Dog Trainers at 800-PET-DOGS.

PRINCIPLES OF TRAINING

Most people think training comprises teaching the dog to do things such as sit, speak and roll over, but

62

even a 4-week-old pup knows how to do these things already. Instead, the first step in training involves teaching the dog human words for each dog behavior and activity and for each aspect of the dog's environment. That way you, the owner, can more easily participate in the dog's domestic education by directing her to perform specific actions appropriately, that is, at the right time, in the right place and so on. Training opens communication channels, enabling an educated dog to at least understand her owner's requests.

In addition to teaching a dog what we want her to do, it is also necessary to teach her why she should do what we ask. Indeed, 95 percent of training revolves around motivating the dog to want to do what we want. Dogs often understand what their owners want; they just don't see the point of doing it—especially when the owner's repetitively boring and seemingly senseless instructions are totally at odds with much more pressing and exciting doggy distractions. It is not so much the dog that is being stubborn or dominant; rather, it is the owner who has failed to acknowledge the dog's needs and feelings and to approach training from the dog's point of view.

The Meaning of Instructions

The secret to successful training is learning how to use training lures to predict or prompt specific behaviors—to coax the dog to do what you want when you want. Any highly valued object (such as a treat or toy) may be used as a lure, which the dog will follow with her eyes and nose. Moving the lure in specific ways entices the dog to move her nose, head and entire body in specific ways. In fact, by learning the art of manipulating various lures, it is possible to teach the dog to assume virtually any body position and perform any action. Once you have control over the expression of the dog's behaviors and can elicit any body position or behavior at will, you can easily teach the dog to perform on request.

Tell your dog what you want her to do, use a lure to entice her to respond correctly, then profusely praise and maybe reward her once she performs the desired action. For example, verbally request "Fido, sit!"

while you move a squeaky toy upwards and backwards over the dog's muzzle (lure-movement and hand signal), smile knowingly as she looks up (to follow the lure) and sits down (as a result of canine anatomical engineering), then praise her to distraction ("Gooood Fido!"). Squeak the toy, offer a training treat and give your dog and yourself a pat on the back.

Being able to elicit desired responses over and over enables the owner to reward the dog over and over. Consequently, the dog begins to think training is fun. For example, the more the dog is rewarded for sitting, the more she enjoys sitting. Eventually the dog comes to realize that, whereas most sitting is appreciated, sitting immediately upon request usually prompts especially enthusiastic praise and a slew of high-level rewards. The dog begins to sit on cue much of the time, showing that she is starting to grasp the meaning of the owner's verbal request and hand signal.

Why Comply?

Most dogs enjoy initial lure-reward training and are only too happy to

Introduce your new puppy to other family pets in a calm and controlled environment.

63

comply with their owners' wishes. Unfortunately, repetitive drilling without appreciative feedback tends to diminish the dog's enthusiasm until she eventually fails to see the point of complying anymore. Moreover, as the dog approaches adolescence she becomes more easily distracted as she develops other interests. Lengthy sessions with repetitive exercises tend to bore and demotivate both parties. If it's not fun, the owner doesn't do it and neither does the dog. Integrate training into your dog's life: The greater number of training sessions each day and the shorter they are, the more willingly compliant your dog will become.

Punishment

Without a doubt, lure-reward training is by far the best way to teach: Entice your dog to do what you want and then reward her for doing so. Unfortunately, a human shortcoming is to take the good for granted and to moan and groan at the bad. Specifically, the dog's many good behaviors are ignored while the owner focuses on punishing the dog for making mistakes. In extreme cases, instruction is limited to punishing mistakes made by a trainee dog, child, employee or husband, even though it has been proven punishment training is notoriously inefficient and ineffective and is decidedly unfriendly and combative. It teaches the dog that training is a drag, almost as quickly as it teaches the dog to dislike her trainer. Why treat our best friends like our worst enemies?

Punishment training is also much more laborious and time-consuming. Whereas it takes only a finite amount of time to teach a dog what to chew, for example, it takes much, much longer to punish the

dog for each and every mistake. Remember, there is only one right way! So why not teach that right way from the outset?!

To make matters worse, punishment training causes severe lapses in the dog's reliability. Since it is obviously impossible to punish the dog each and every time she misbehaves, the dog quickly learns to distinguish between those times when she must comply (so as to avoid impending punishment) and those times when she need not comply, because punishment is impossible. Such times include when the dog is off leash and 6 feet away, when the owner is otherwise engaged (talking to a friend, watching television, taking a shower, tending to the baby or chatting on the telephone) or when the dog is left at home alone.

Instances of misbehavior will be numerous when the owner is away, because even when the dog complied in the owner's looming presence, she did so unwillingly. The dog was forced to act against her will, rather than molding her will to want to please. Hence, when the owner is absent, not only does the dog know she need not comply, she simply does not want to. Again, the trainee is not a stubborn vindictive beast, but rather the trainer has failed to teach. Punishment training invariably creates unpredictable Jekyll and Hyde behavior.

TRAINER'S TOOLS

Many training books extol the virtues of a vast array of training paraphernalia. In reality, most effective training tools are not found in stores; they come from within ourselves. In addition to a willing dog, all you really need is a functional human brain, gentle hands, a loving heart and a good attitude.

In terms of equipment, all dogs do require a quality buckle collar to sport dog tags and to attach the leash (for safety and to comply with local leash laws). Hollow chew toys (like Kongs or sterilized longbones) and a dog bed or collapsible crate are musts for housetraining. Three additional tools are required:

1. specific lures (training treats and toys) to predict and prompt specific desired behaviors;

2. rewards (praise, affection, training treats and toys) to reinforce for the dog what a lot of fun it all is; and

3. knowledge—how to convert the dog's favorite activities and games (potential distractions to training) into "life-rewards," which may be employed to facilitate training.

The most powerful of these is knowledge. Education is the key!

HOUSETRAINING

If dogs were left to their own devices, certainly they would chew, dig and bark for entertainment and then no doubt highlight a few areas

65

A good-quality leash will be an integral part of the dog training process.

Use newspaper to begin the process of house-training your puppy.

of their living space with sprinkles of urine, in much the same way we decorate by hanging pictures. Consequently, when we ask a dog to live with us, we must teach her *where* she may dig, *where* she may perform her toilet duties, *what* she may chew and *when* she may bark. After all, when left at home alone for many hours, we cannot expect the dog to amuse herself by completing crosswords or watching the soaps on TV!

Also, it would be decidedly unfair to keep the house rules a secret from the dog, and then get angry and punish the poor critter for inevitably transgressing rules she did not even know existed. Remember: Without adequate education and

guidance, the dog will be forced to establish her own rules—doggy rules—and most probably will be at odds with the owner's view of domestic living.

Since most problems develop during the first few days the dog is at home, prospective dog owners must be certain they are quite clear about the principles of housetraining *before* they get a dog. Early misbehaviors quickly become established as the *status quo*—becoming firmly entrenched as hard-to-break bad habits, which set the precedent for years to come. Make sure to teach your dog good habits right from the start. Good habits are just as hard to break as bad ones!

Ideally, when a new dog comes home, try to arrange for someone to be present as much as possible during the first few days (for adult dogs) or weeks for puppies. With only a little forethought, it is surprisingly easy to find a puppy sitter, such as a retired person, who would be willing to eat from your refrigerator and watch your television while keeping an eye on the newcomer to encourage the dog to play with chew toys and to ensure she goes outside on a regular basis.

Potty Training

To teach the dog where to relieve herself:

1. never let her make a single mistake;

2. let her know where you want her to go; and

3. handsomely reward her for doing so: "GOOOOOOOD DOG!!!" liver treat, liver treat, liver treat!

Preventing Mistakes

A single mistake is a training disaster, since it heralds many more in future weeks. And each time the dog soils the house, this further reinforces the dog's unfortunate preference for an indoor, carpeted toilet. Do not let an unhousetrained dog have full run of the house.

When you are away from home, or cannot pay full attention, confine the dog to an area where elimination is appropriate, such as an outdoor run or, better still, a small, comfortable indoor kennel with access to an outdoor run. When confined in this manner, most dogs will naturally housetrain themselves.

If that's not possible, confine the dog to an area, such as a utility room, kitchen, basement or garage, where elimination may not be desired in the long run, but as an interim measure it is certainly preferable to doing it all around the house. Use newspaper to cover the floor of the dog's day room. The newspaper may be used to soak up the urine and to wrap up and dispose of the feces. Once your dog develops a preferred spot for eliminating, it is only necessary to cover that part of the floor with newspaper. The smaller papered area may then be moved (only a little each day) towards the door to the outside. Thus the dog will develop the tendency to go to the door when she needs to relieve herself.

Never confine an unhousetrained dog to a crate for long periods. Doing so would force the dog to soil the crate and ruin its usefulness as an aid for housetraining (see the following discussion).

Teaching Where

In order to teach your dog where you would like her to do her business, you have to be there to direct

67

the proceedings—an obvious, yet often neglected, fact of life. In order to be there to teach the dog where to go, you need to know *when* she needs to go. Indeed, the success of housetraining depends on the owner's ability to predict these times. Certainly, a regular feeding schedule will facilitate prediction somewhat, but there is nothing like "loading the deck" and influencing the timing of the outcome yourself!

Whenever you are at home, make sure the dog is under constant supervision and/or confined to a small area. If already well trained, simply instruct the dog to lie down in her bed or basket. Alternatively, confine the dog to a crate (doggy den) or tie-down (a short, 18-inch lead that can be clipped to an eye hook in the baseboard near her bed). Short-term close confinement strongly inhibits urination and defecation, since the dog does not want to soil her sleeping area. Thus, when you release the puppydog each hour, she will definitely need to urinate immediately and defecate every third or fourth hour. Keep the dog confined to her doggy den and take her to her intended toilet area each hour, every hour, on the hour. When taking your dog outside, instruct her

to sit quietly before opening the door—she will soon learn to sit by the door when she needs to go out!

Teaching Why

Being able to predict when the dog needs to go enables the owner to be on the spot to praise and reward the dog. Each hour, hurry the dog to the intended toilet area in the yard, issue the appropriate instruction ("Go pee!" or "Go poop!"), then give the dog three to four minutes to produce. Praise and offer a couple of training treats when successful. The treats are important because many people fail to praise their dogs with feeling . . . and housetraining is hardly the time for understatement. So either loosen up and enthusiastically praise that dog: "Wuzzzer-wuzzer-wuzzer, hoooser good wuffer den? Hoooo went pee for Daddy?" Or say "Good dog!" as best you can and offer the treats for effect.

Following elimination is an ideal time for a spot of play-training in the yard or house. Also, an empty dog may be allowed greater freedom around the house for the next half hour or so, just as long as you keep an eye out to make sure she does not get into other kinds of mischief. If you are preoccupied and cannot pay full attention, confine the dog to her doggy den once more to enjoy a peaceful snooze or to play with her many chew toys.

If your dog does not eliminate within the allotted time outside—no biggie! Back to her doggy den, and then try again after another hour.

Beware of falling into the trap of walking the dog to get her to eliminate. The good ol' dog walk is such an enormous highlight in the dog's life that it represents the single biggest potential reward in domestic dogdom. However, when in a hurry, or during inclement weather, many owners abruptly terminate the walk the moment the dog has done her business. This, in effect, severely punishes the dog for doing the right thing, in the right place at the right time. Consequently, many dogs become strongly inhibited from eliminating outdoors because they know it will signal an abrupt end to an otherwise thoroughly enjoyable walk.

Instead, instruct the dog to relieve herself in the yard prior to going for a walk. You will find with a "No feces—no walk" policy, your dog will become one of the fastest defecators in the business.

A baby gate will come in handy when you want to keep your dog confined to one part of the house.

If you do not have a backyard, instruct the dog to eliminate right outside your front door prior to the walk. Not only will this facilitate clean up and disposal of the feces in your own trash can, but, also, the walk may again be used as a colossal reward.

CHEWING AND BARKING

Short-term close confinement also teaches the dog that occasional quiet moments are a reality of domestic living. Your puppydog is extremely impressionable during her first few weeks at home. Regular confinement at this time soon exerts a calming influence over the dog's personality. Remember, once the dog is housetrained and calmer, there will be a whole lifetime ahead for the dog to enjoy full run of the house and garden. On the other hand, by letting the newcomer have unrestricted access to the entire household and allowing her to run willy-nilly, she will most certainly develop a bunch of behavior problems in short order, no doubt necessitating confinement later in life.

When confining the dog, make sure she always has an impressive array of suitable chew toys. Kongs and sterilized longbones (both readily available from pet stores) make the best chew toys, since they are hollow and may be stuffed with treats to heighten the dog's interest.

Remember, treats do not have to be junk food and they certainly should not represent extra calories. Rather, treats should be part of each dog's regular daily diet: Some food may be served in the dog's bowl for breakfast and dinner, some food may be used as training treats and some food may be used for stuffing chew

Making sure your dog has proper chew toys will help you train her not to chew on your furniture.

70

toys. I regularly stuff my dogs' many Kongs with different shaped biscuits and kibble. The kibble seems to fall out fairly easily, as do the oval-shaped biscuits, thus rewarding the dog instantaneously for checking out the chew toys. The bone-shaped biscuits fall out after a while, rewarding the dog for worrying at the chew toy. But the triangular biscuits never come out. They remain inside the Kong as lures, maintaining the dog's fascination with her chew toy. To further focus the dog's interest, I always make sure to flavor the triangular biscuits by rubbing them with a little cheese or freeze-dried liver.

If stuffed chew toys are reserved especially for times the dog is confined, the puppydog will soon learn to enjoy quiet moments in her doggy den and she will quickly develop a chew-toy habit—a good habit! This is a simple autoshaping process; all the owner has to do is set up the situation and the dog all but trains herself—easy and effective. Even when the dog is given run of the house, her first inclination will be to indulge her rewarding chew-toy habit rather than destroy less attractive household articles, such as curtains, carpets, chairs and

compact disks. Similarly, a chew-toy chewer will be less inclined to scratch and chew herself excessively. Also, if the dog busies herself as a recreational chewer, she will be less inclined to develop into a recreational barker or digger when left at home alone.

Stuff a number of chew toys whenever the dog is left confined and remove the extra-special-tasting treats when you return. Your dog will now amuse herself with her chew toys before falling asleep and then resume playing with her chew toys when she expects you to return. Since most owner-absent misbehavior happens right after you leave and right before your expected return, your puppydog will now be conveniently preoccupied with her chew toys at these times.

COME AND SIT

Most puppies will happily approach virtually anyone, whether called or not; that is, until they collide with adolescence and develop other more important doggy interests, such as sniffing a multiplicity of exquisite odors on the grass. Your mission, Mr./Ms. Owner, is to teach and reward the pup for coming reliably, willingly and happily when called—and you have just three months to get it done. Unless adequately reinforced, your puppy's tendency to approach people will self-destruct by adolescence.

Call your dog ("Fido, come!"), open your arms (and maybe squat down) as a welcoming signal, waggle a treat or toy as a lure and reward the puppydog when she comes running. Do not wait to praise the dog until she reaches you—she may come 95 percent of the way and then run off after some distraction. Instead, praise the dog's first step towards you and continue praising enthusiastically for every step she takes in your direction.

When the rapidly approaching puppydog is three lengths away from impact, instruct her to sit ("Fido, sit!") and hold the lure in front of you in an outstretched hand to prevent her from hitting you mid-chest and knocking you flat on your back! As Fido decelerates to nose the lure, move the treat upwards and backwards just over her muzzle with an upwards motion of your extended arm (palm-upwards). As the dog looks up to follow the lure, she will sit down (if she jumps up, you are

holding the lure too high). Praise the dog for sitting. Move backwards and call her again. Repeat this many times over, always praising when Fido comes and sits; on occasion, reward her.

For the first couple of trials, use a training treat both as a lure to entice the dog to come and sit and as a reward for doing so. Thereafter, try to use different items as lures and rewards. For example, lure the dog with a Kong or Frisbee but reward her with a food treat. Or lure the dog with a food treat but pat her and throw a tennis ball as a reward. After just a few repetitions, dispense with the lures and rewards; the dog will begin to respond willingly to your verbal requests and hand signals just for the prospect of praise from your heart and affection from your hands.

Instruct every family member, friend and visitor how to get the dog to come and sit. Unless you teach your dog how to meet people, that is, to sit for greetings, no doubt the dog will resort to jumping up. Then you and the visitors will get annoyed, and the dog will be punished. This is not fair.

Even though your dog quickly masters obedient recalls in the

To teach come, call your dog, open your arms as a welcoming signal, wave a toy or a treat and praise for every step in your direction.

house, her reliability may falter when playing in the backyard or local park. Ironically, it is the owner who has unintentionally trained the dog not to respond in these instances. By allowing the dog to play and run around and otherwise have a good time, but then to call the dog to put her on leash to take her home, the dog quickly learns playing is fun but training is a drag. Thus, playing in the park becomes a severe distraction, which works against training. Bad news!

Instead, whether playing with the dog off leash or on leash, request her to come at frequent intervals— say, every minute or so. On most occasions, praise and pet the dog for a few seconds while she is sitting, then tell her to go play again. For especially fast recalls, offer a couple of training treats and take the time to praise and pet the dog enthusiastically before releasing her. The dog will learn that coming when called is not necessarily the end of the play session, and neither is it the end of the world; rather, it signals an enjoyable, quality time-out with the owner before resuming play once more. In fact, playing in the park now becomes a very effective life-reward, which works to facilitate training by reinforcing each obedient and timely recall. Good news!

SIT, DOWN, STAND AND ROLL OVER

Teaching the dog a variety of body positions is easy for owner and dog, impressive for spectators and extremely useful for all. Using lure-reward techniques, it is possible to train several positions at once to verbal commands or hand signals (which impress the socks off of onlookers).

Sit and down—the two control commands—prevent or resolve nearly a hundred behavior problems. For example, if the dog happily and obediently sits or lies down when requested, she cannot jump on visitors, dash out the front door, run around and chase her tail, pester other dogs, harass cats or annoy family, friends or strangers. Additionally, "Sit" or "Down" are the best emergency commands for off-leash control.

It is easier to teach and maintain a reliable sit than maintain a reliable recall. Sit is the purest and simplest of commands—either the dog is sitting or she is not. If there is any change of circumstances or potential danger in the park, for example, simply instruct the dog to sit. If she sits, you have a number of options: Allow the dog to resume playing when she is safe, walk up and put the dog on leash or call the dog. The dog will be much more likely to come when called if she has already acknowledged her compliance by sitting. If the dog does not sit in the park—train her to!

Stand and roll over-stay are the two positions for examining the dog. Your veterinarian will love you to distraction if you take a little time to teach the dog to stand still and roll over and play possum.

As with teaching come and sit, the training techniques to teach the dog to assume all other body positions on cue are user-friendly and dog-friendly. Simply give the appropriate request, lure the dog into the desired body position using a training treat or toy and then praise (and maybe reward) the dog as soon as she complies. Try not to touch the dog to get her to respond. If you teach the dog by guiding her into position, the dog will quickly learn that rump-pressure means sit, for example, but as yet you still have no control over your dog if she is just 6 feet away. It will still be necessary to teach the dog to sit on request. So do not make training a time-consuming two-step process; instead, teach the dog to sit to a verbal request or hand signal from the outset. Once the dog sits willingly when requested, by all means use your hands to pet the dog when she does so.

To teach down when the dog is already sitting, say "Fido, down!," hold the lure in one hand (palm down) and lower that hand to the floor between the dog's forepaws. As the dog lowers her head to follow the lure, slowly move the lure away from the dog just a fraction (in front of her paws). The dog will lie down as she stretches her nose forward to follow the lure. Praise the dog when she does so. If the dog stands up, you pulled the lure away too far and too quickly.

When teaching the dog to lie down from the standing position, say "Down" and lower the lure to the floor as before. Once the dog has lowered her forequarters and assumed a play bow, gently and slowly move the lure towards the dog between her forelegs. Praise the dog as soon as her rear end plops down.

You will notice the more energetically you move your arm—upwards (palm up) to get the dog to sit, and downwards (palm down) to get the dog to lie down—the more energetically the dog responds to your requests. Now try training the dog in silence and you will notice she has also learned to respond to hand signals. Yeah! Not too shabby for the first session.

To teach stand from the sitting position, say "Fido, stand," slowly move the lure half a dog-length away from the dog's nose, keeping it at nose level, and praise the dog as she stands to follow the lure. As soon as the dog stands, lower the lure to just beneath the dog's chin to entice her to look down; otherwise she will stand and then sit immediately. To prompt the dog to stand from the down position, move the lure half a dog-length upwards and away from the dog, holding the lure at standing nose height from the floor.

Teaching roll over is best started from the down position, with the dog lying on one side, or at least with both hind legs stretched out on the same side. Say "Fido, bang!" and move the lure backwards and alongside the dog's muzzle to her elbow (on the side of her outstretched hind legs). Once the dog looks to the side and backwards, very slowly move the lure upwards to the dog's shoulder and backbone. Tickling the dog

Using a food
lure to teach sit,
down and stand.
1) "Phoenix, sit."
2) Hand palm
upwards, move
lure up and
back over dog's
muzzle.
3) "Good sit,
Phoenix!"

4) "Phoenix,
down."
5) Hand palm
downwards,
move lure down
to lie between
dog's forepaws.
6) "Phoenix, off.
Good down,
Phoenix!"

7) "Phoenix, sit!"
8) Palm
upwards, move
lure up and
back, keeping it
close to dog's
muzzle.
9) "Good sit,
Phoenix!"

10) *"Phoenix, stand!"*
11) *Move lure away from dog at nose height, then lower it a tad.*
12) *"Phoenix, off! Good stand, Phoenix!"*

13) *"Phoenix, down!"*
14) *Hand palm downwards, move lure down to lie between dog's forepaws.*
15) *"Phoenix, off! Good down-stay, Phoenix!"*

77

16) *"Phoenix, stand!"*
17) *Move lure away from dog's muzzle up to nose height.*
18) *"Phoenix, off! Good stand-stay, Phoenix. Now we'll make the vet and groomer happy!"*

in the goolies (groin area) often invokes a reflex-raising of the hind leg as an appeasement gesture, which facilitates the tendency to roll over. If you move the lure too quickly and the dog jumps into the standing position, have patience and start again. As soon as the dog rolls onto her back, keep the lure stationary and mesmerize the dog with a relaxing tummy rub.

To teach roll over-stay when the dog is standing or moving, say "Fido, bang!" and give the appropriate hand signal (with index finger pointed and thumb cocked in true Sam Spade fashion), then in one fluid movement lure her to first lie down and then roll over-stay as above.

Teaching the dog to stay in each of the above four positions becomes a piece of cake after first teaching the dog not to worry at the toy or treat training lure. This is best accomplished by hand feeding dinner kibble. Hold a piece of kibble firmly in your hand and softly instruct "Off!" Ignore any licking and slobbering for however long the dog worries at the treat, but say "Take it!" and offer the kibble *the instant* the dog breaks contact with

her muzzle. Repeat this a few times, and then up the ante and insist the dog remove her muzzle for one whole second before offering the kibble. Then progressively refine your criteria and have the dog not touch your hand (or treat) for longer and longer periods on each trial, such as for two seconds, four seconds, then six, ten, fifteen, twenty, thirty seconds and so on.

The dog soon learns: (1) worrying at the treat never gets results, whereas (2) noncontact is often rewarded after a variable time lapse.

Teaching "Off!" has many useful applications in its own right. Additionally, instructing the dog not to touch a training lure often produces spontaneous and magical stays. Request the dog to stand-stay, for example, and not to touch the lure. At first set your sights on a short two-second stay before rewarding the dog. (Remember, every long journey begins with a single step.) However, on subsequent trials, gradually and progressively increase the length of stay required to receive a reward. In no time at all your dog will stand calmly for a minute or so.

RELEVANCY TRAINING

Once you have taught the dog what you expect her to do when requested to come, sit, lie down, stand, roll over and stay, the time is right to teach the dog why she should comply with your wishes. The secret is to have many (many) extremely short training interludes (two to five seconds each) at numerous times during the course of the dog's day. In no time at all the dog will be only too pleased to follow your instructions because she has learned that a compliant response heralds all sorts of goodies. Basically all you are trying to teach the dog is how to say please: "Please throw the tennis ball. Please may I snuggle on the couch."

In fact, the dog may be unable to distinguish between training and good times, and, indeed, there should be no distinction. The warped concept that training involves forcing the dog to comply and/or dominating her will is totally at odds with the picture of a truly well-trained dog. In reality, enjoying a game of training with a dog is no different from enjoying a game of backgammon or tennis with a friend; and

walking with a dog should be no different from strolling with a spouse, or with buddies on the golf course.

WALK BY YOUR SIDE

Many people attempt to teach a dog to heel by putting her on a leash and physically correcting the dog when she makes mistakes. There are a number of things seriously wrong with this approach, the first being that most people do not want precision heeling; rather, they simply want the dog to follow or walk by their side. Second, when physically restrained during "training," even though the dog may grudgingly mope by your side when "handcuffed" on leash, let's see what happens when she is off leash. History! The dog is in the next county because she never enjoyed walking with you on leash, and you have no control over her off leash. So let's just teach the dog off leash from the outset to want to walk with us. Third, if the dog has not been trained to heel, it is a trifle hasty to think about punishing the poor dog for making mistakes and breaking heeling rules she didn't even know existed. This is simply not fair! Surely, if the dog had been adequately taught how to heel, she would seldom make mistakes and hence there would be no need to correct the dog. Remember, each mistake and each correction (punishment) advertise the trainer's inadequacy, not the dog's. The dog is not stubborn, she is not stupid and she is not bad. Even if she were, she would still require training, so let's train her properly.

Let's teach the dog to enjoy following us and to want to walk by our side off leash. Then it will be easier to teach high-precision off-leash heeling patterns if desired. Before going on outdoor walks, it is necessary to teach the dog not to pull. Then it becomes easy to teach on-leash walking and heeling because the dog already wants to walk with you, she is familiar with the desired walking and heeling positions and she knows not to pull.

FOLLOWING

Start by training your dog to follow you. Many puppies will follow if you simply walk away from them and maybe click your fingers or chuckle.

Adult dogs may require additional enticement to stimulate them to follow, such as a training lure or, at the very least, a lively trainer. To teach the dog to follow: (1) keep walking and (2) walk away from the dog. If the dog attempts to lead or lag, change pace; slow down if the dog forges too far ahead, but speed up if she lags too far behind. Say "Steady!" or "Easy!" each time before you slow down and "Quickly!" or "Hustle!" each time before you speed up, and the dog will learn to change pace on cue. If the dog lags or leads too far, or if she wanders right or left, simply walk quickly in the opposite direction and maybe even run away from the dog and hide.

Practicing is a lot of fun; you can set up a course in your home, yard or park to do this. Indoors, entice the dog to follow upstairs, into a bedroom, into the bathroom, downstairs, around the living room couch, zigzagging between dining room chairs and into the kitchen for dinner. Outdoors, get the dog to follow around park benches, trees, shrubs and along walkways and lines in the grass. (For safety outdoors, it is advisable to attach a long line on the dog, but never exert corrective tension on the line.)

Remember, following has a lot to do with attitude—your attitude! Most probably your dog will not want to follow Mr. Grumpy Troll with the personality of wilted lettuce. Lighten up—walk with a jaunty step, whistle a happy tune, sing, skip and tell jokes to your dog and she will be right there by your side.

BY YOUR SIDE

It is smart to train the dog to walk close on one side or the other—either side will do, your choice. When walking, jogging or cycling, it is generally bad news to have the dog suddenly cut in front of you. In fact, I train my dogs to walk "By my side" and "Other side"—both very useful instructions. It is possible to position the dog fairly accurately by looking to the appropriate side and clicking your fingers or slapping your thigh on that side. A precise positioning may be attained by holding a training lure, such as a chew toy, tennis ball, or food treat. Stop and stand still several times throughout the walk, just as you would when window shopping or meeting a friend. Use the lure to make sure the dog slows down and stays close whenever you stop.

81

Like many other breeds, well-trained Rottweilers can be used as therapy dogs.

When teaching the dog to heel, we generally want her to sit in heel position when we stop. Teach heel position at the standstill and the dog will learn that the default heel position is sitting by your side (left or right—your choice, unless you wish to compete in obedience trials, in which case the dog must heel on the left).

Several times a day, stand up and call your dog to come and sit in heel position—"Fido, heel!" For example, instruct the dog to come to heel each time there are commercials on TV, or each time you turn a page of a novel, and the dog will get it in a single evening.

Practice straight-line heeling and turns separately. With the dog sitting at heel, teach her to turn in place. After each quarter-turn, half-turn or full turn in place, lure the dog to sit at heel. Now it's time for short straight-line heeling sequences, no more than a few steps at a time. Always think of heeling in terms of sit-heel-sit sequences—start and end with the dog in position and do your best to keep her there when moving. Progressively increase the number of steps in each sequence. When the dog remains close for 20 yards of straight-line

heeling, it is time to add a few turns and then sign up for a happy-heeling obedience class to get some advice from the experts.

NO PULLING ON LEASH

You can start teaching your dog not to pull on leash anywhere—in front of the television or outdoors—but regardless of location, you must not take a single step with tension in the leash. For a reason known only to dogs, even just a couple of paces of pulling on leash is intrinsically motivating and diabolically rewarding. Instead, attach the leash to the dog's collar, grasp the other end firmly with both hands held close to your chest and stand still—do not budge an inch. Have somebody watch you with a stopwatch to time your progress. Otherwise, you will never believe this will work, and so you will not even try the exercise, and your shoulder and the dog's neck will be traumatized for years to come.

Stand still and wait for the dog to stop pulling and to sit and/or lie down. All dogs stop pulling and sit eventually. Most take only a couple of minutes; the all-time record is

$22^1/_2$ minutes. Time how long it takes. Gently praise the dog when she stops pulling, and as soon as she sits, enthusiastically praise the dog and take just one step forwards, then immediately stand still. This single step usually demonstrates the ballistic reinforcing nature of pulling on leash; most dogs explode to the end of the leash, so be prepared for the strain. Stand firm and wait for the dog to sit again. Repeat this half a dozen times, and you will probably notice a progressive reduction in the force of the dog's one-step explosions and a radical reduction in the time it takes for the dog to sit each time.

As the dog learns "Sit we go" and "Pull we stop," she will begin to walk forward calmly with each single step and automatically sit when you stop. Now try two steps before you stop. Wooooooo! Scary! When the dog has mastered two steps at a time, try for three. After each success, progressively increase the number of steps in the sequence: Try four steps and then six, eight, ten and twenty steps before stopping. Congratulations! You are now walking the dog on leash.

Whenever walking with the dog (off leash or on leash), make sure you stop periodically to practice a few position commands and stays before instructing the dog to "Walk on!" (Remember, you want the dog to be compliant everywhere, not just in the kitchen when her dinner is at hand.) For example, stopping every 25 yards to briefly train the dog amounts to over 200 training interludes within a single 3-mile stroll. And each training session is in a different location. You will not believe the improvement within just the first mile of the first walk.

To put it another way, integrating training into a walk offers 200 separate opportunities to use the continuance of the walk as a reward to reinforce the dog's education. Moreover, some training interludes may comprise continuing education for the dog's walking skills: Alternate short periods of the dog walking calmly by your side with periods when the dog is allowed to sniff and investigate the environment. Now sniffing odors on the grass and meeting other dogs become rewards that reinforce the dog's calm and mannerly demeanor. Good Lord! Whatever next? Many enjoyable walks together, of course. Happy trails!

CHAPTER NINE

Further Reading

BOOKS

About Rottweilers

Brace, Andrew, ed. *The Ultimate Rottweiler.* New York: Howell Book House, 1995.

Elsden, Judy and Larry. *The Rottweiler Today.* New York: Howell Book House, 1992.

Freeman, Muriel. *The Complete Rottweiler.* New York: Howell Book House, 1984.

MacPhail, Mary. *Pet Owner's Guide to the Rottweiler.* New York: Howell Book House, 1993.

About Health Care

American Kennel Club. *American Kennel Club Dog Care and Training.* New York: Howell Book House, 1991.

Carlson, Delbert, DVM, and James Giffen, MD. *Dog Owner's Home Veterinary Handbook.* New York: Howell Book House, 1992.

DeBitetto, James, DVM, and Sarah Hodgson. *You & Your Puppy.* New York: Howell Book House, 1995.

Humphries, Jim, DVM. *Dr. Jim's Animal Clinic for Dogs.* New York: Howell Book House, 1994.

Schwartz, Stefanie, DVM. *First Aid for Dogs: An Owner's Guide to a Happy Healthy Pet.* New York: Howell Book House, 1998.

Smith, Cheryl S. *Pudgy Pooch, Picky Pooch.* Hauppage, N.Y.: Barron's Educational Series, Inc., 1998.

About Dog Shows

Coile, Caroline D., PhD *Show Me!* Hauppage, N.Y.: Barron's Educational Series, Inc., 1997.

Hall, Lynn. *Dog Showing for Beginners.* New York: Howell Book House, 1994.

About Training

Ammen, Amy. *Training in No Time.* New York: Howell Book House, 1995.

Benjamin, Carol Lea. *Dog Problems.* New York: Howell Book House, 1989.

Dunbar, Ian, PhD, MRCVS. *Dr. Dunbar's Good Little Book.* James & Kenneth Publishers, 2140 Shattuck Ave. #2406, Berkeley, Calif. 94704. (510) 658-8588. Order from publisher.

———. *How to Teach a New Dog Old Tricks.* James & Kenneth Publishers. Order from the publisher; address above.

Dunbar, Ian, PhD, MRCVS, and Gwen Bohnenkamp. *Booklets on Preventing Aggression; Housetraining; Chewing; Digging; Barking; Socialization; Fearfulness; and Fighting.* James & Kenneth Publishers. Order from the publisher; address above.

Evans, Job Michael. *People, Pooches and Problems.* New York: Howell Book House, 1991.

About Activities

American Rescue Dog Association. *Search and Rescue Dogs*. New York: Howell Book House, 1991.

Barwig, Susan and Stewart Hilliard. *Schutzhund*. New York: Howell Book House, 1991.

Davis, Kathy Diamond. *Therapy Dogs*. New York: Howell Book House, 1992.

Holland, Vergil S. *Herding Dogs*. New York: Howell Book House, 1994.

Neil, Jackie. *All About Agility*. New York: Howell Book House, 1998.

Volhard, Jack and Wendy. *The Canine Good Citizen*. New York: Howell Book House, 1994.

GENERAL TITLES

Fogel, Bruce, DVM. *The Dog's Mind: Understanding Your Dog's Behavior*. New York: Howell Book House, 1990.

Haggerty, Captain Arthur J. *How to Get Your Pet Into Show Business*. New York: Howell Book House, 1994.

McLennan, Bardi. *Dogs and Kids, Parenting Tips*. New York: Howell Book House, 1993.

Sife, Wallace, PhD. *The Loss of a Pet*, New Revised Edition. New York: Howell Book House, 1998.

Wrede, Barbara J. *Civilizing Your Puppy*. Hauppauge, N.Y.: Barron's Educational Series, Inc., 1992.

MAGAZINES

THE AKC GAZETTE
The Official Journal for the Sport of Purebred Dogs
American Kennel Club
51 Madison Ave.
New York, NY 10010

DOG FANCY
Fancy Publications
3 Burroughs
Irvine, CA 92718

DOG WORLD
Maclean Hunter Publishing Corp.
29 N. Wacker Dr.
Chicago, IL 60606

RESOURCES

The American Kennel Club

The American Kennel Club, devoted to the advancement of purebred dogs, is the oldest and largest registry organization in this country. Every breed recognized by the AKC has a national (parent) club. National clubs are a great source of information on your breed. The affiliated clubs hold AKC events and use AKC rules to hold performance events, dog shows, educational programs, health clinics and training classes. The AKC staff is divided between offices in New York City and Raleigh, North Carolina. All registration functions are done in North Carolina.

For registration and performance events information, contact:
THE AMERICAN KENNEL CLUB
5580 Centerview Drive, Suite 200
Raleigh, NC 27606
Phone: (919) 233-9767
Fax: (919) 233-3627
E-mail: info@akc.org

For obedience information, contact:
THE AMERICAN KENNEL CLUB
51 Madison Ave.
New York, NY 10010

Phone: (212) 696-8276
Fax: (212) 696-8272
E-mail: www.akc.org

For information on AKC Companion Animal Recovery, contact:
Phone: (800) 252-7894
Fax: (919) 233-1290
E-mail: found@akc.org

Registry Organizations

Registry organizations register purebred dogs.

UNITED KENNEL CLUB (UKC)
100 E. Kilgore Rd.
Kalamazoo, MI 49002

AMERICAN DOG BREEDERS ASSOCIATION
180 U.S. Hwy. 89
Salt Lake City, UT 84054
(Registers American Pit Bull Terriers)

CANADIAN KENNEL CLUB
100-89 Skyway Ave.
Etobicoke, Ontario
Canada M9W 6R4

NATIONAL STOCK DOG REGISTRY
P.O. Box 402
Butler, IN 46721
(Registers working stock dogs)

ORTHOPEDIC FOUNDATION FOR ANIMALS (OFA)
2300 E. Nifong Blvd.
Columbia, MO 65201-3856
(Hip registry)

Activity Clubs

Write to these organizations for information on the activities they sponsor.

UNITED KENNEL CLUB
100 E. Kilgore Rd.
Kalamazoo, MI 49002
(Conformation Shows, Obedience Trials, Agility, Hunting for Various Breeds, Terrier Trials and more.)

INTERNATIONAL SLED DOG RACING ASSOCIATION
P.O. Box 446
Nordman, ID 83838

Trainers

ASSOCIATION OF PET DOG TRAINERS
P.O. Box 385
Davis, CA 95617
800-PET-DOGS

MORE INFORMATION ON ROTTWEILERS

National Breed Club

AMERICAN ROTTWEILER CLUB
Doreen LePage, Secretary
960 South Main St.
Pascoag, RI 02859
The club can give you information on all aspects of the breed, including the names and addresses of breed, obedience and herding clubs in your area. Inquire about membership.

Magazines

THE ARC, A Publication of the American Rottweiler Club
Marilyn Piusz
339 Co. Hwy. 106
Johnstown, NY 12095-9730

THE ROTTWEILER QUARTERLY
GRQ Publications
3355 Conant Lane
Watsonville, CA 95076

Videos

Rottweilers. The American Kennel Club.

ESSENTIAL ROTTWEILER QUICK REFERENCE CARD

Your Dog's Name _____

Name on Your Dog's Pedigree (if applicable) _____

Where Your Dog Was Purchased _____

    Address _____

    Phone Number _____

Your Dog's Birthday _____

Your Dog's Veterinarian _____

    Address _____

    Phone Number _____

    Emergency Number _____

Your Dog's Health

    VACCINES

      Type _____ *Date Given* ___/___/___

      Type _____ *Date Given* ___/___/___

      Type _____ *Date Given* ___/___/___

      Type _____ *Date Given* ___/___/___

    HEARTWORM

      Date Tested ___/___/___   *Type Used* _____ *Start Date* ___/___/___

Your Dog's License Number _____

Groomer's Name and Phone Number _____

Dog Sitter/Walker's Name and Phone Number _____

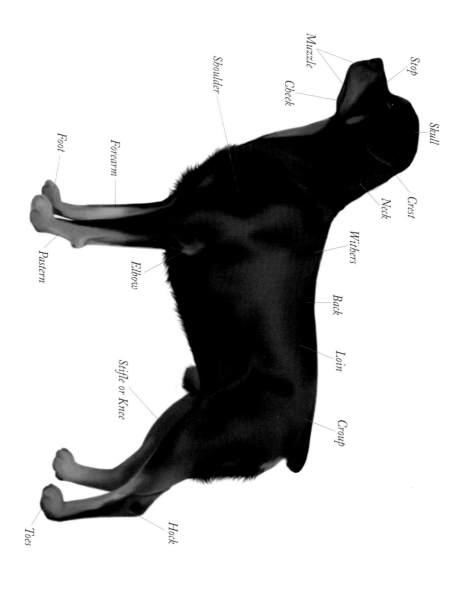

EXTERNAL FEATURES OF A ROTTWEILER

Muzzle

Stop

Cheek

Skull

Shoulder

Crest

Neck

Foot

Withers

Forearm

Back

Pastern

Elbow

Loin

Stifle or Knee

Croup

Toes

Hock